Multiethnic Conversations is another example of Marl
how to build bridges in practical ways with theological
a "gracist" who understands that comprehension beg
church sponsors *Multiethnic Conversations* for the sak

—DAVID ANDERSON, founder and senior pastor of Bridgeway Community Church in Col........

Every church intentionally moving into a "church like heaven" (Rev. 7:9) future will reach a point where meaningful conversations across racial, ethnic, and cultural lines are essential. This tool beautifully provides how to do just that. We know from local church experience how much a relationally based and Bible-rooted small group curriculum such as this can provide a deeper, more authentic diverse unity and inclusion for your congregation. I'm so grateful to Mark and Oneya for producing this crucial life primer for the church of Jesus Christ.

—CHRISTOPHER N. BEARD, lead pastor of Peoples Church in Cincinnati, executive presbyter, Assemblies of God, Ohio Ministry Network

At first I found it useful for me and my own journey, but soon it became one of the best resources I've used with my church and now my entire denomination for leaders and laity at every level. It not only helps to start discussions and create safe space for more in-depth conversations, but it also gives common language and a common experience for those wanting to not only do multiethnic ministry effectively, but who want to authentically lead multiethnic lives as well.

—SANTES BEATTY, director of multi-ethnic ministries of The Wesleyan Church

Our church has used this material to engage over fifty families from fifteen different birth nations to start the discussions of how we "walk, work, and worship together." One of the key elements of developing a multiethnic ministry is establishing multicultural competence. Mark DeYmaz and Oneya Fennell Okuwobi have provided the tool we have used to accomplish that goal. I recommend this work to all pastors and teachers pursuing the biblical goal of multicultural ministry.

—MARK HEARN, senior pastor of First Baptist Church in Duluth, GA and author of *Technicolor: Inspiring Your Church to Embrace Multicultural Ministry* (coming soon by B&H Publishing)

Becoming a multiethnic church often feels like an ethereal goal that is just out of reach. Mark and Oneya have crafted a tangible guide to help you have the necessary conversations to take a step forward in this journey of becoming a multiethnic church. Do this with your small group and your church to spark a multiethnic movement in your city.

—DANIEL IM, coauthor of *Planting Missional Churches* and director of Church Multiplication for NewChurches.com

Oneya Fennell Okuwobi is not only one of the leading scholars of multiethnic congregational development, she is also a leading practitioner. As a leader at Peoples Church in Cincinnati, she has been a critical part of the team that has helped the church move from a monolithic White congregation, to one of the most vibrant multiethnic congregations in America. Okuwobi's commitment to effective biblically rooted conversations has led to both growing racial reconciliation and a broadening commitment to racial and economic justice in the public square. This study is a treasure rooted in the lived experience and wisdom of its author.

—TROY JACKSON, coauthor of *Forgive Us: Confessions of a Compromised Faith* and director of The AMOS Project in Cincinnati, OH

MULTIETHNIC CONVERSATIONS

AN EIGHT-WEEK JOURNEY TOWARD UNITY IN YOUR CHURCH

MARK DeYMAZ
ONEYA FENNELL OKUWOBI

wesleyan
PUBLISHING HOUSE
wphstore.com

Copyright © 2016 by Mark DeYmaz and Oneya Fennell Okuwobi
Published by Wesleyan Publishing House
Indianapolis, Indiana 46250
Printed in the United States of America
ISBN: 978-1-63257-095-6
ISBN (e-book): 978-1-63257-097-0

This book is revised from the work previously published as *The Mult-Ethnic Christian
Life Primer*, by Mosaix Global Network, 2013, United States of America.

Library of Congress Cataloging-in-Publication Data

DeYmaz, Mark, 1961- author.
Multiethnic conversations : an eight-week journey toward unity in your
   church / Mark DeYmaz, Oneya Fennell Okuwobi.
Indianapolis : Wesleyan Publishing House, 2016. I Includes
   bibliographical references.
LCCN 2016033869 I ISBN 9781632570956 (concealed coil)
LCSH: Church and minorities--Textbooks. I Ethnicity--Religious
   aspects--Christianity--Textbooks. I Multiculturalism--Religious
   aspects--Christianity--Textbooks.
LCC BV639.M56 D496 2016 I DDC 259.089--dc23 LC record available at https://lccn.
loc.gov/2016033869

CONTENTS

For additional free resources,
visit wphresources.com/multiethnic.

INTRODUCTION

All over the United States and across the world, Christ-followers are embracing a vision that reflects God's heart for all people, beyond race, class, and cultural distinctions. Yet, few tools exist to teach diverse groups of believers how to walk, work, and worship God together as one in the local church for the sake of the gospel. For this reason, we have written *Multiethnic Conversations*. Based on Oneya's groundbreaking work at Peoples Church of Cincinnati, Ohio, and Mark's teaching at Mosaic Church of Central Arkansas in Little Rock, this is the first individual daily and small-group study on multiethnic life and church designed not only for pastoral leaders, but also—especially—for people in the pews.

To be clear, this study is not at all like typical "diversity" training you may have had at work or school. Rather, it is rooted in God's Word. As such, it focuses on reconciling diverse men and women with God, and consequently with one another, through faith in Jesus Christ. It also inspires local churches to embrace the principles and practices of New Testament multiethnic churches that existed at Antioch, Ephesus, and Rome.

Through this eight-week daily journey, you will come to understand the biblical mandate for the multiethnic church, and gain practical insights for experiencing life with diverse others in the body of Christ. Each week begins with a study of theological truth (day one), specifically the concept of unity as central to the character of God, and an imperative to the local church. On days two and three, a study of history and demographics will provide context for understanding theological truth in light of the church and culture today. Next, by considering cross-cultural relationships, communication skills, and cross-cultural competence (days four through six), you will discover what it takes to develop transparency and trust across the distinctions of this world that so often and otherwise divide people. Finally, each chapter ends with a biblical reflection (day seven), providing opportunities for the Spirit of God to further enlighten your mind, heart, and soul.

Much more than a simple devotional, *Multiethnic Conversations* can and should be used as a small-group curriculum. In fact, we recommend that you gather a diverse group of people each week to discuss the readings and questions that you will otherwise consider alone. When using the material in a small-group context, do not be afraid to share, especially when your thinking runs contrary to what you are hearing from others involved. Varied viewpoints engage and enliven everyone, especially when shared with love, sensitivity, and respect. As others share, you may hear comments or stories that seem very foreign to you. In such moments, listen respectfully and carefully to gain insight into another's life experience, perhaps one very different than your own. Indeed, there is something to learn from everyone, no matter who they are or where they have come from.

Pastors, too, can use this material as the basis for an eight-week sermon series. When they do, the entire church will exponentially gain from simultaneous interaction with this study's concepts at three levels: as individuals, in small groups, and from the large-group setting.

Finally, keep in mind that the topics raised here will not always be comfortable for you to consider; few things are comfortable when dealing with issues of ethnicity, class, and culture. But even when this study gets difficult, we encourage you to lean in and keep going. The rewards of new understanding and relationships will be well worth it.

So let's start the conversation!

WEEK 1

WHY MULTIETHNIC?

• • ● • •

THEOLOGY

Jesus taught us to pray, "Your kingdom come, your will be done, on earth as it is in heaven" (Matt. 6:10). According to Revelation 7:9, in heaven there will be "a great multitude that no one [can] count, from every nation, tribe, people and language, standing before the throne [of God] and before the Lamb [Jesus]." So here's the question: If the kingdom of heaven is not segregated, why on earth is the local church?

Consider:

- Jesus *envisioned* the multiethnic church, for the sake of the gospel, on the night before he died (John 17:2–3, 20–23).
- Luke *described* the multiethnic church in action, at Antioch, as a model for future congregations to follow (Acts 11:19–26; 13:1–3).
- Paul *prescribed* the multiethnic church in order to advance a credible witness of God's love for all people (Eph. 2:11—4:6; 3:2, 6).

Pursuit of a multiethnic church and, likewise, a multiethnic Christian life, must be firmly rooted in God's Word; racism is ultimately a spiritual problem. As history proves time and again, no earthly attempt relying on human effort, can truly change the heart. Only God can do this, and will do this, when we allow the Spirit to speak to us through Scripture.

When diverse men and women have been reconciled with God through faith in Jesus Christ, they are to be collectively reconciled with one another in and through the local church (see Eph. 2:11—4:6); and the local church, itself, reconciled with the principles and practices of New Testament local churches, such as existed at Antioch, Ephesus, and Rome. These early churches were truly diverse communities of faith in which believing Jews and Gentiles walked, worked, and worshiped God, together as one so that the world would know God's love and believe (John 17:23).

Thus, the local churches in the New Testament were characterized by:

- Men and women of varying ethnic and economic backgrounds;
- Walking, working, and worshiping God, together as one;
- Providing a credible witness of God's love for all people in a diverse society;
- Obeying the Great Commandment, demonstrating great compassion, and fulfilling the Great Commission;
- Resulting in a great expansion of the gospel, local church, and kingdom of God.

JOURNAL

• • ● • •

Would you describe the churches you've attended as typically segregated along ethnic and economic lines or diverse? What do you think has made them so? If more segregated, does that bother you? Why or why not?

What are some reasons that local churches tend to segregate along ethnic and economic lines?

What excites you about the possibilities of experiencing a multiethnic church and living the multiethnic Christian life?

What fears or concerns might you have in doing so?

DAY 2
HISTORY

"Eleven o'clock on Sunday morning is the most segregated hour of the week."

Most people attribute this observation to Dr. Martin Luther King Jr. However, as noted religious scholar, Dr. Martin Marty pointed out, the observation was first made toward the end of the nineteenth century. Concerning that period in American history, Marty wrote, "White Protestants . . . did little to build bonds with [Black Protestant] churches, and racially there were at least two Americas or Christianities. Doctrinal and practical similarity counted for little. . . . Critics noted that the Sunday Protestant worship hour was the most segregated time of the week. Indeed, the once righteous churches of the North, after proclaiming triumph over the evils of slavery and the South, came during the next century to adopt Southern styles of regard for Blacks and their churches, and there was little positive contact even within denominational families."[1]

Surely it breaks God's heart that so many churches throughout the country are still segregated by race and class. More than that, the very gospel itself is unintentionally undermined when it's proclaimed from segregated pulpits and pews. The fact is, there is no clearer or more credible witness of God's love for all people than the witness of diverse believers walking, working, and worshiping God, together as one in and through the local church. The advance of the church and the gospel in the twenty-first century depends upon passionate and purposeful individuals getting this right.

JOURNAL

• • ● • •

In this season of your life, what has shaped your interest in the multiethnic church and living a multiethnic Christian life?

Considering how diverse the church you currently attend or lead is, what's making it so diverse, or perhaps keeping diverse others from getting involved?

What are some ways you could gain insights into what might make more diverse groups of people feel welcome at and comfortable in your church?

CONSIDERATIONS

During each week of this study, the third day, titled "Considerations," invites you to explore some key statistics, concepts, and truths significant to this discussion. Today provides a chance to learn about the demographic makeup of the United States. As you read the facts below, see if any seem surprising, and think about how closely your church mirrors the larger society.

- As of April 30, 2016, the United States had a total resident population of 323,730,000.
- There were 125.9 million females in the United States in 2014. The number of males was 119.4 million.
- The national median age was 36.8 years in 2009.
- The United States Census Bureau defines White people as those "having origins in any of the original peoples of Europe, the Middle East, or North Africa. It includes people who reported 'white' or wrote in entries such as Irish, German, Italian, Lebanese, Near Easterner, Arab, or Polish." According to the 2010 United States Census, Whites currently constitute the majority of the US population, with a total of 223,553,265 or 72.4 percent of the population.
- Currently, population growth is fastest among minorities as a whole, and according to the Census Bureau's estimation for 2012,

50.4 percent of American children under the age of one belonged to minority groups.

- Hispanic and Latino Americans accounted for 69 percent of the national population growth of 2.9 million between July 1, 2005, and July 1, 2006. Immigrants and their US-born descendants are expected to provide most of the US population gains in the decades ahead.[2]
- According to the latest projections by demographers and social scientists, by 2042, the United States will be a majority-minority nation in which there will be more collective minorities than the historically White majority.[3]
- Minority children will be the majority of kids in the entire United States by 2019.[4]

JOURNAL

• ● ●

As you think about the ethnic and cultural shifts predicted for our society, how do you think the church should respond, if at all? What might happen if the church doesn't respond?

Consider the following statement that Mark wrote to explain why I (Oneya) believe a multiethnic life and church is vital:

> "I'm not out promoting the multiethnic church or pursuing a multiethnic Christian life because of changing demographics or because Rodney King once asked us all to get along. I'm doing so because it is biblical, it's right, and it's the hope of the gospel in an increasingly diverse and cynical society."

In the space below, write your own initial statement as to why you believe the local church should not be segregated. (Be prepared to add to or adjust this statement as your understanding grows over the next several weeks.)

DAY 4
RELATIONSHIPS

In their book *Divided by Faith*, sociologists Michael Emerson and Christian Smith share their findings that local churches in America are actually perpetuating systemic inequities in society. Their research not only confirmed that most evangelicals attend racially segregated churches, but also that they spend 70–80 percent of their time relationally with others who attend the same local church as they do. The conclusion is this: Evangelical Christians today are not only *racially* segregated from one another, they are *relationally* segregated from one another as well.[5]

Q: How does the racial and relational segregation of Christians in America perpetuate systemic inequities in society?

A: Apart from ethnically and economically diverse relationships we cannot grow in our understanding of others different from ourselves; we cannot develop trust with others different from ourselves; we will not truly love others different from ourselves. Apart from understanding, trust, and love, we are less likely to engage with others different from ourselves, or to address the systemic inequalities and racial realities so often experienced by minorities throughout America. And without such involvement, nothing changes: systemic inequities are perpetuated, and the disparaging consequences of institutional racism remain deeply entrenched in our society.

Q: What is institutional (or systemic) racism?

A: "The collective failure of an organization to provide an appropriate and professional service to people because of their color, culture, or ethnic origin. It can be seen and detected in processes, attitudes, and behaviors, which amount to discrimination through unwitting prejudice, ignorance, thoughtlessness, and racist stereotyping, which disadvantage minority ethnic people."[6]

Institutional Racism describes any system that exists in which the effects of racism are felt or experienced by individuals within it, and where the cause of these effects is not overt racism (or racist intent). So even if no one *means* to treat people from other ethnic or economic groups differently, or even realizes that they are, if they *do* treat them differently, racism still exists.

JOURNAL

• • ● • •

Name three people (outside your family) with whom you share the closest relationships. How many of these relationships began in your local church? How many of these three people are of a different ethnicity and/or economic background than you?

What have you experienced in developing cross-cultural relationships so far? What would you say are the benefits and/or challenges involved in doing so?

Have you seen examples of institutional racism? Explain the situation.

COMMUNICATION

Stay within your own cultural tribe and space, and make disciples of people that are just like you refers to the "Not-So-Great Commission." Fortunately, this is not at all what Jesus had in mind, or commanded his followers to do (see Matt. 28:19–20).

Rather, he commanded us to leave what is otherwise culturally comfortable and live a Christian life filled with a wide array of people in order to make disciples, no matter who they are or from where they have come. Interacting positively with diverse people—whether at home or abroad—will require us to improve cross-cultural communication skills, and you can do this in a healthy multiethnic church. If we're not willing to communicate with the diverse people across the street, what makes us think we can do so across an ocean?

Historically, significant misunderstandings have developed because people mistranslate the words or actions of others, or even entire cultures, because they read them through their own personal or cultural lenses. This has been well documented on the mission field. For example, in polite cultures such as that of the Makhuwa of Northern Mozambique, villagers may respond to an invitation to receive Christ simply because they don't want to be rude. In such circumstances, missionaries must be able to communicate well with indigenous leaders who can then, in turn, disciple their own people to an authentic commitment to Christ.

In the same way, pursuit of a multiethnic Christian life can help us learn to understand the difference between what is being said and what we are hearing when we interact with those from ethnic or social backgrounds different from our own. Learning to truly communicate cross-culturally allows us to develop authentic, transparent, and trust-filled relationships across cultural divides. In a healthy multiethnic church, we can learn the unspoken rules of other cultures as well as how to avoid frustrations or hurt feelings.

JOURNAL

Have you ever had a disagreement, frustration, or hurt involving someone of a different race or ethnic background that can be attributed to miscommunication? If so, what did you experience? How was the situation resolved?

Looking back, what could you have done to prevent miscommunication?

If you have ever spent time traveling or living in another culture, describe the barriers or challenges to communication you experienced.

How did your understanding of the culture, or lack of it, help or hurt you in overcoming any obstacles to communication?

COMPETENCE

"If one part suffers, every part suffers with it; if one part is honored, every part rejoices with it" (1 Cor. 12:26).

In this verse, the apostle Paul described in part what it means to be the family of God and, more specifically, part of a local church family in which the members both know and are known by one another. Of course, in any family, members develop a deep and personal understanding of one another. Since the family of God includes brothers and sisters who are ethnically, economically, and culturally different from one another, the pursuit of cross-cultural competence is required of everyone involved in a healthy multiethnic church or who lives a multiethnic Christian life. (*Competence* refers to proficiency in addressing another's culture or customs, needs, and expectations when they differ from our own. It means becoming adept in the idiosyncrasies of language and learning the ins and outs of traditions of others.)

Take a look at this cross-cultural continuum:

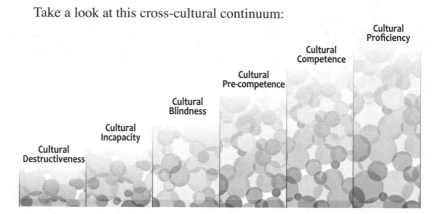

When considering or interacting with people of varied cultural backgrounds, many at first find themselves in a stage of either blindness or pre-competence. Those who are culturally blind treat everyone the same and expect everyone to think, behave, and respond the same without regard to cultural differences that exist. When people move into pre-competence, they develop an awareness of cultural differences and needs, but don't really know what to do with it.

However, in a healthy multiethnic church, members pursue cross-cultural competence and proficiency. As outlined by Bonita Williams in *The Journal of Extension,* cross-cultural competence includes:

- *Self-knowledge/awareness*: Because so much of the culture we know is subconscious, self-awareness starts the process by enabling us to consciously understand our own cultural biases and how they might impact others.
- *Experience with others from another culture*: Personal interactions with diverse people, and gaining knowledge about their culture(s), enables us to develop a relationship through which we can enter into their experience.
- *Positive change or action leading to successful interaction with another culture*: Those who are cross-culturally competent have made changes and/or refined their actions to maximize, both in quantity and quality,

interactions with others from another culture. The full richness and benefit of these relationships then thrives.[7]

JOURNAL

● ● ● ● ●

MY PERSONAL EXPERIENCE SURVEY
Check the boxes that apply to you.

Personal Experiences	Whites	Blacks	Asians	Latinos	Others
I have worked on teams with					
I have worked for					
I have managed					
I have gone to lunch with					
I have sought out for personal advice					
I have been mentored by					
I have spent time discussing my faith with					
I have had in my home as part of a larger group					
I have had in my home as individuals or a family					
I have seen films about					
I have read books about					
My children regularly play with					
I grew up in a neighborhood with					
My current neighbors include					
My social circles include					
I have close friends who are					
I have taken a vacation with					
I have had in my home overnight					
I have been discriminated by					
I have been criminally victimized by					
I have been emotionally hurt by					

Answer the following questions based on your survey responses:
Were you surprised by the results? If so, in what way(s)?

With which groups have you had the most and least interaction? Why?

Would you say that you've had significant interactions outside your own cultural group? What has encouraged or prevented this?

What differences would you like to see if you took this survey one year from now?

DAY 7

REFLECTION

As you read the following verses, ask the Lord to speak to your heart through them, based on what you've been learning.

My prayer is not for them alone. I pray also for those who will believe in me through their message, that all of them may be one, Father, just as you are in me and I am in you. May they also be in us so that the world may believe that you have sent me. I have given them the glory that you gave me, that they may be one as we are one—I in them and you in me—so that they may be brought to complete unity. Then the world will know that you sent me and have loved them even as you have loved me. (John 17:20–23)

On the night before Jesus died, he revealed to us the most effective means for reaching the world with the gospel: be one . . . so that the world will know God's love and believe.

JOURNAL

• • ● • •

Write a prayer inspired by the verses you just read.

WEEK 2

WHY NOW?

• • ● • •

THEOLOGY

The apostle Paul's explanation of the gospel in the book of Romans has been well studied, taught, and celebrated. Much less, however, is understood about why Paul had to explain the gospel to the Romans in the first place. In short, following the death of the Roman emperor Claudius (AD 59), Jewish believers, who had been scattered for a time, once again joined Gentiles in the church at Rome. How then were the two groups to live as one in Christ and in the church; and more importantly, why? Some background on the opening verses of Paul's letter to Rome will help explain.

First, Paul establishes his authority and calling as an apostle set apart for the gospel of God (Rom. 1:1–4). Next, he explains his own unique mission within that assignment: "To call all the Gentiles to the obedience that comes through faith . . ." (Rom. 1:5). In other words, yes, Paul was writing to explain the gospel, but more than that, he was writing to address the implications of the gospel; namely, the concept of Gentile inclusion in what may otherwise have become an all-Jewish gospel, local church, and kingdom of God.

Over and over throughout Romans, Paul pairs these two concerns: teaching the gospel and clarifying its individual and collective impact. For him the gospel of Jesus Christ and the concept of Gentile inclusion are two sides of the same coin. Read the following passages and see for yourself:

- Romans 1:16
- Romans 3:21–22, 29–30
- Romans 10:9, 11–13
- Romans 15:15–16
- Romans 16:25–26

In Paul's view, Gentile inclusion is inextricably linked to the gospel (Rom. 16:25–26); not simply as the gospel pertains to eternal life, but where development of the local church on earth is concerned as well.

Somewhat troubled by this teaching on Gentile inclusion, a pastor in Phoenix once asked Mark, "Isn't the gospel enough?" In other words, he was suggesting that by simply preaching the gospel, diverse people will be moved to walk, work, and worship God together as one in the local church. Yet in spite of resurgence in gospel preaching today, 86 percent of churches throughout the United States remain segregated at present, failing to have at least 20 percent diversity in their attending membership. So we should honestly ask, "How's that working for us?" The reality is that even after being reconciled with God through faith in Christ, we have much work to do, and many challenges to overcome, in order to be reconciled with one another.

Similarly, another pastor objected that in advocating for multiethnic church communities, "it seems you are elevating diversity over the gospel." Yet, as just observed in the book of Romans, Paul was both clear and intentional in calling attention to this implication of the gospel: namely, in expecting that local churches would be multiethnic and economically diverse, wherever possible, in order to present a credible witness of the very gospel itself to a diverse society. In response, then, it's not about elevating one (diversity) over the other (the gospel). It's about understanding that the two were inextricably linked in Paul's mind. Therefore, they should be linked in our minds too.

The most prominent leaders in the American church today do not have any problem addressing with intentionality New Testament truths related to church planting, growth, and development. Through writing, speaking, and teaching, these leaders rightly call Christ-centered believers, and the local churches they attend, to be intentional in their evangelism, discipleship, worship, small group involvement, local and foreign missions, and more. So why should any of these leaders shy away from addressing New Testament expectations concerning unity and diversity in the local church with equal intention and passion, for the sake of the gospel?

JOURNAL

• • ● • •

How would you respond to the question, "Isn't the gospel enough?" In other words, do you think it's reasonable to expect that in merely hearing the gospel diverse people will come together as one in the local church? Explain your answer.

Do you think intentional teaching from the New Testament that expects both unity and diversity in the local church detracts from or enhances gospel proclamation today? Explain your answer.

DAY 2

HISTORY

In future weeks, we'll continue to look further into the history of relations between the various ethnicities, races, cultures, and social groups in American society. Let's pause a moment now, however, to consider how history may inform such relations today.

The day after a jury in Sanford, Florida, found George Zimmerman not guilty in the shooting death of Trayvon Martin on February 26, 2012, *USA Today*'s front-page story headline asked, "After Zimmerman Verdict, Can Nation Heal Racial Rift?"[1] The years since have seen very little healing and much more violence. The controversial deaths of Michael Brown, Eric Garner, Tamir Rice, Sandra Bland, Sam Dubose, Freddie Gray, John Crawford, Renisha McBride, and others have spurred the birth of the Black Lives Matter movement. Along with these events has come an increased volume of painful questions about race.

As we face these profound questions that will impact our society's future, this question is increasingly relevant: Can America's racial rift(s) be healed?

In a word: perhaps. But not until we as multiethnic Christians, local church pastors, church planters, and denominational leaders take seriously the need to address systemic segregation within our own local congregations. Racism is ultimately a spiritual problem. Consequently, systemic racial inequities in society cannot be righted until they are first righted in the church.

Think about it. The American church has virtually no credibility in society's eyes when it comes to addressing the racial rifts, systemic inequities, and cultural divides that deeply affect the United States today. Our absence from the discussion, however, cannot be blamed on the media. Rather, our lack of credibility and collective irrelevance are the result of our own failures when it comes to building cross-cultural relationships, pursuing cross-cultural competence, and promoting a spirit of inclusion within the local church.

In 2013, President Barack Obama asserted, "The larger discussion of race belongs not with lawmakers in Washington but in living rooms, houses of worship, and workplaces."[2] And Dr. John M. Perkins, reflecting on young people today, noted, "This is the first generation that values diversity."[3]

To explain, while some members of previous generations nobly fought for minorities' equal treatment, equal rights, and integrated communities, diversity today is viewed almost universally as a positive thing. When this view for diverse relationships is combined with a desire to see all equally valued in every interaction, that's valuing diversity in its deepest sense. It's where true and lasting change can happen. It's a matter of the heart, hands, and spirit. The time then is now to embrace the vision of the multiethnic church and pursue a multiethnic Christian life for the sake of Christ and community.

JOURNAL

• • ● • •

The acquittal verdicts handed down in the historic trials of O. J. Simpson and George Zimmerman were largely praised and condemned along racial lines. Be honest: Why do you think this was so?

What message does a segregated church send to the larger society? What message does a multiethnic church send?

DAY 3
CONSIDERATIONS

Census information, when combined with church attendance and other records, offers thought-provoking insights into what is happening in churches today. As you read the statistics below, take time to consider what each one means for the church as a whole, especially for churches in poorer, urban, or multiethnic communities. What impact does this have on churches within each of the various communities mentioned? How might God want churches from within the various communities to respond?

- Between 1990 and 2009, the United States population grew by 56,819,471 people.[4]
- Between 1990 and 2009 church attendance in the United States grew by 446,540 people (less than 1 percent of the total population growth).[5]
- Between 2000 and 2009, evangelical churches in zip codes with an Anglo population of less than 79 percent declined in attendance by an average of 1.9 percent. Meanwhile evangelical churches in zip codes with an Anglo population more than 80 percent grew by an average of 3.2 percent.[6]
- Between 2000 and 2009, evangelical churches whose members earned a median income of less than 40,000 dollars averaged 92 people in size, while evangelical churches whose members earned a median income of more than 40,000 dollars averaged 180 people in size.[7]

- Between 2000 and 2009, evangelical churches whose members had a median education level of less than one year of college declined by an average of 2 percent, while evangelical churches whose members had a median education level of more than one year of college or more grew by an average of 5.2 percent.[8]

JOURNAL

• • ● • •

In the above statistics, what trends do you see when it comes to church growth among the various communities? How might they impact diversity?

With these statistics in mind, in an increasingly diverse and cynical society, would the local church be seen as more or less relevant to our culture today? Why? Would those outside the church be more or less inclined to believe the church's message? Why?

What do the statistics cited concerning the impact of Anglo population by zip code, as well as median income and education by zip code, suggest to you about the effectiveness of evangelical church planting, growth, and development as it exists in the United States today?

RELATIONSHIPS

True or false? Most adults are terrible listeners.

In a study conducted at Carnegie Mellon University, researchers asked test subjects to listen to a ten-minute talk. Moments after the talk, only 50 percent could describe what they had just heard. Within 48 hours, only 25 percent could even recall the subject matter! This is because while the fastest speakers use only about 125 words per minute, "the human brain has the capacity to digest as much as 400 words per minute of information." What this means is that 75 percent of our brain is probably elsewhere when others are speaking.[9] Despite such challenges, in order to live a multiethnic Christian life, you'll need to become a good listener.

How can I become unified with a diverse group of people in and through the local church? Oneness with others who are different from us begins with a commitment to pursue cross-cultural relationships. This means taking the time to understand the cultural perspectives, history, and struggles of people groups beyond our own. This requires us to listen and really hear others different than ourselves.

The goal of cross-cultural interaction is not to get others to think, feel, or become like us; it is to listen and to learn about and from them. In so doing, we should we not force the discussion. Rather, we must be patient in the beginning and throughout the entire process of establishing these relationships. In addition, we must love, serve, and give of ourselves too.

Over time, God will bring to light even more significant questions, needs, or hurts that we can further process together as we grow deeper as one. Above all, pray that God will lead you in this regard. In the end, only the Holy Spirit can cleanse the mind, heal damaged emotions, and provide strength for the will to overcome the pain of negative past experiences rooted in racial or class prejudice.

JOURNAL

• • ● • •

What are two or three ways in which you might push yourself to become a better listener?

What is the most fulfilling cross-cultural relationship you have, or have had in the past, with someone of a different race, ethnicity, or socio-economic class? Why was this particular relationship so meaningful to you?

COMMUNICATION

In recent years, a cultural spotlight has shone on the social divisions in America. We've talked red states versus blue states, Wall Street versus Main Street, and past generations versus today's generation in an effort to measure the divides. We even have separate news outlets geared toward political preference.

Take a look at the graph below.[10] It shows one such area of division: trust of the government by political party.

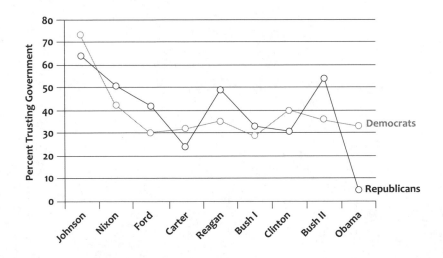

Notice that over the past twelve years, Democrats and Republicans have been at least fifteen points apart in the percentage of those in their respective parties who say they trust the government. Interestingly, this widening gap appears after having remained within a fairly narrow band for the previous thirty years. The more recent separation tells us that divisions are growing among us. And these divisions will remain until we learn to communicate with diverse others more effectively.

Have you ever heard an evening newscast describing a united Christian viewpoint on any subject or issue? In all probability, you haven't. More likely, you've heard various viewpoints qualified by terms such as "White evangelical," or "Black Protestant." The reason for the distinction is that these two groups are typically divided in their perspective and opinion on many current issues. For example, 95 percent of Black Protestants voted democratic in the 2008 and 2012 presidential elections compared to less than 25 percent of White evangelicals.[11] And the list goes on.

Ask yourself:

- Could a more united and persuasive Christian point of view be presented to the world if these two groups walked, worked, and worshiped God together as one: living from Sunday to Sunday as part of one local church, sitting side by side in the same pews, listening to the same sermon, learning from and communicating well with one another, in a spirit of brotherly love and mutual respect?
- Would a united front lead to a more credible witness of the gospel in an otherwise polarized society, provide a more reasoned peace in the midst of contentious debate, and show the world a more excellent way (1 Cor. 12:31)?

Instead of condemning the things that divide, those who pursue a multi-ethnic Christian life choose to focus on the points of connection that we share in common. As believers, and by demonstrating respectful patterns of cross-cultural communication, we can play a key role in helping to heal divisions in America.

In this regard, our primary point of connection is the gospel: namely, our faith in the Lord Jesus Christ who lived, died, and rose again to give eternal life to all those who believe in him. When we *will* ourselves to walk, work, and worship God together as one in a local church, we become bright lights in the public square and model the peace of Christ that passes human understanding—the very peace for which the world longs.

JOURNAL

• • ● • •

Recall a time when you tried to communicate with someone who didn't seem to be listening. How did this make you feel?

Imagine a newspaper reporting on diverse members of a multiethnic church speaking with one voice to a particular need or issue affecting the community and how they are significantly impacting public opinion. Write the headline below:

DAY 6
COMPETENCE

As important as it is to listen to one another, it is equally important to understand that there can be a difference between what is being said and what we are hearing. The other person may intend to communicate one thing by their words or actions, but we may think they are saying something else entirely. This is particularly true when speaking and listening across cultural lines.

To better understand this, consider the disparity in the following comments paraphrased from Facebook posts addressing Michelle Obama's means and motives in establishing the "Let's Move" program to combat childhood obesity.

Critics of the program said:

- "The government just needs to stay out of the private sector's business! They can't tell us what to do and what and how much to eat! Who do they think they are? They all need to be kicked out of office!"
- "I determine what my kids eat; I am their mom, not Michelle Obama."

But supporters of the program heard:

- "I do not like the Obamas; there is nothing they do that is good."
- "You shouldn't expect any help from the government. You're on your own in life."

Supporters of the program said:

* "Lots of neighborhoods lack healthy food options. I'm glad something is being done so more people have access to fruits and vegetables."
* "You are seriously criticizing the First Lady's anti-obesity message? Seriously? Do you know that obesity in children has decreased since she started this program?"

But critics of the program heard:

* "It's the government's job to provide what we need, so we don't have to do it ourselves."
* "The 'nanny state' isn't bad, even if it means higher taxes and more regulations. The government knows better than we do and should tell us how to live, rather than allow us freedom."

In this example, from what was being said and heard, it's easy to see how miscommunication and misunderstanding developed in the absence of genuine relationships of transparency and trust between critics and supporters. If genuine relationships existed between those trying to communicate their opinions, how might their conversation have developed in a more positive direction?

Let's also consider some of the more common statements made between diverse individuals, otherwise trying to pursue cross-cultural competence, that have been known to cause conflict.

Your Black friends will not likely want to hear:

* America is a Christian nation.
* If there's a Black History Month, why isn't there a White History Month?
* One of my best friends is Black.
* I don't see color.

Your White friends will not likely want to hear:

* You don't know what it is to struggle.
* You're a racist because you're White.
* You owe Black people an apology.
* People don't succeed because the system is stacked against them.

Your Latino friends will not likely want to hear:

* I know some Guatemalan Mexicans; what kind of Mexican are you?
* When did you come to America?
* Wow, you speak good English!
* Are you legal?

Your Asian friends will not likely want to hear:

* What kind of Asian are you?
* Where are you from . . . no, like, really from?
* I love Bruce Lee movies!
* Can you fix my computer?

While such statements may be well-intentioned and true for the person speaking them, it's easy to see how they can damage cross-cultural interaction. Therefore it's critical to pursue cross-cultural competence in order to better understand others who differ from us and to avoid offense, even unintentionally, in our relationships. Even when cross-cultural relationships have matured, we should continue to share our opinions in such a way as to be heard by others, even when disagreeing. Grace, love, and respect go a long way toward positive, productive interactions, perhaps most especially when disagreements arise.

JOURNAL

• • ● • •

Write down any other phrases common to your experience that annoy you personally.

Take a moment to further consider the phrases you wrote down. In fairness, what might you imagine the speakers are really trying to say?

REFLECTION

As you read the following verses, ask the Lord to speak to your heart through them, based on what you've been learning.

On one occasion, an expert in the law stood up to test Jesus, "Teacher," he asked, "what must I do to inherit eternal life?"

"What is written in the Law?" he replied. "How do you read it?"

He answered, "'Love the Lord your God with all your heart and with all your soul and with all your strength and with all your mind'; and, 'Love your neighbor as yourself.'"

"You have answered correctly," Jesus replied. "Do this and you will live."

But the man wanted to justify himself, so he asked Jesus, "And who is my neighbor?"

In reply Jesus said: "A man was going down from Jerusalem to Jericho, when he was attacked by robbers. They stripped him of his clothes, beat him and went away, leaving him half dead. A priest happened to be going down the same road, and when he saw the man, he passed by on the other side. So too, a Levite, when he came to the place and saw him, passed by on the other side. But a Samaritan, as he traveled, came where the man was; and when he saw him, he took pity on him. He went to him and bandaged his wounds, pouring on oil and wine. Then he put the man on his own donkey, brought him to an inn and took care of him. The next day he took out two denarii and gave them to the innkeeper. 'Look after him,' he said, 'and when I return, I will reimburse you for any extra expense you may have.'

"Which of these three do you think was a neighbor to the man who fell into the hands of robbers?"

The expert in the law replied, "The one who had mercy on him."

Jesus told him, "Go and do likewise." (Luke 10:25–37)

JOURNAL

Write a prayer inspired by the verses you just read.

WEEK 3

OBSTACLES TO DATE

• • ● • •

THEOLOGY

In Matthew 28:19, Jesus commanded his disciples, "Therefore go and make disciples of all nations." But have you ever wondered why we must read eight chapters into the book of Acts before finding anyone who actually leaves Jerusalem for the sake of the gospel? Like many today, it seems the early disciples found it difficult to leave the environment they knew best.

If Jesus commanded them to go, why did they stay?

From Abram's wanderings to a place far from his home, to Joseph sent to the land of Egypt; from Ruth leaving for Bethlehem, to Christ himself, it's hard to find anyone of significant influence in the Bible who was not first called to leave someone or someplace behind in order to become all that God intended them to be, or do all that God intended them to do.

Likewise, in order to live a multiethnic Christian life, we must be willing to go. We must be willing to leave the comfort and familiarity of homogeneity in order to develop cross-cultural relationships and pursue cross-cultural competence. We must be willing to walk, work, and worship God together as one with others different than ourselves; and we must be willing not only to look out for our own personal interests, but also the interest of others (Phil. 2:4).

Did you know that the first church to collect donations for those in need beyond its walls was the church at Antioch (Acts 11:28–30)? Furthermore, it was not the homogeneous church in Jerusalem, but the multiethnic church at Antioch that first mobilized its people and sent missionaries to the world in response to the Great Commission (Acts 13:2–3). In fact, not one but three missionary journeys were launched from Antioch. Consequently, the gospel spread throughout all of Asia Minor and into Europe as well.[1] Let's imagine how this might have happened.

People of varying ethnic and cultural backgrounds—converted Jews and Gentiles alike—filled the church at Antioch (Acts 11:19–20). Many of them had been drawn to the bustling city from all over the known world for business and other reasons. Having then received Christ, these new, diverse believers would have soon considered their mothers and fathers, sisters and brothers, extended family members and friends, still living in the lands from which they came. They would have desired for their loved ones to receive the gift of eternal life.

So why did the church at Antioch care about the world? Because the people there reflected the world! They were a multiethnic congregation that considered it essential to send its money, men, and message of hope abroad to family, friends, and countrymen in obedience to Christ (Matt. 28:19–20; Acts 1:8). For them, involvement in missions was not programmatic, but personal. It reflected who they were, as it will in any church where diverse people are seeking to live a multiethnic Christian life.

JOURNAL

• • ● • •

Describe an experience in which you had to leave your own comfort zone to engage someone (or others) cross-culturally.

What were some of the challenges you faced in so doing, and how did you overcome them?

Draw a picture that best describes the community in which you live in terms of its diversity. How would you explain what you've drawn to others?

Draw a picture that best describes the church you currently attend in terms of its diversity. How would you explain what you drew to others?

HISTORY

While some denominations have been multiethnic at times in their history, most have fractured through the years. Bowing to personalities, personal preferences, theological differences, and shifting societal norms, ethnic and economic segregation in these denominations, and the churches they spawned, became the standard.

Consider the following three examples:

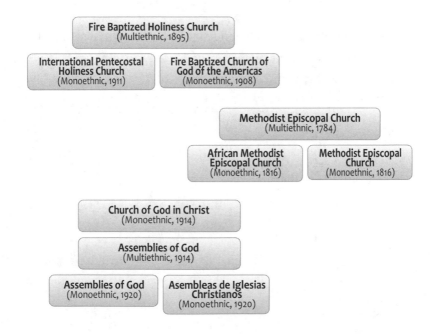

Fire Baptized Holiness Church
(Multiethnic, 1895)

International Pentecostal Holiness Church
(Monoethnic, 1911)

Fire Baptized Church of God of the Americas
(Monoethnic, 1908)

Methodist Episcopal Church
(Multiethnic, 1784)

African Methodist Episcopal Church
(Monoethnic, 1816)

Methodist Episcopal Church
(Monoethnic, 1816)

Church of God in Christ
(Monoethnic, 1914)

Assemblies of God
(Multiethnic, 1914)

Assemblies of God
(Monoethnic, 1920)

Asembleas de Iglesias Christianos
(Monoethnic, 1920)

JOURNAL

· · ● · ·

What do you imagine were some of the obstacles these denominations faced in attempting to remain multiethnic? What kinds of pressures might a multiethnic group experience that make it difficult to stay together? How might such issues be overcome?

Take a moment to research online the history of your denomination or church and its past concerning matters of diversity. In the space below, write down what you discover.

CONSIDERATIONS

Admittedly racism is a charged, tough-to-talk-about subject in American life and culture. However, those who desire a multiethnic Christian life cannot ignore it. Nor can we talk about building healthy multiethnic churches without addressing it on some level. The fact is, racism has contributed to the systemic segregation of local churches throughout the United States for well over one hundred years.

It is commonly believed that racism, or even racial separation, is an innate part of human nature, but this is not the case. In fact, in addressing this topic, it's worth noting that while discrimination between ethnic groups and cultures has a long history, racism is a relatively new phenomenon. "Social oppression based on human groupings has always been part of our societies, but until recently, this oppression has not generally been linked to notions of physical distinctions. If we define racism as creating or maintaining racial group inequality and justifying that inequality, then racism may not have begun to develop until the emergence of the Atlantic slave trade."[2]

Another example of the recent development of race is found in the book *White by Law*. Author Ian Haney Lopez described the history of court cases wherein immigrants sued to be recognized as White, and therefore eligible for naturalization. These were not straightforward decisions. In 1894, a law review article asserted "that Japanese immigrants were eligible for citizenship on the grounds that the Japanese people were anthropologically and culturally white."[3] As this illustrates, who qualifies as White, Black, or another race is not determined as much by biology as we might at first presume. It is determined by social agreement and has been shaped by the law.

This modern racism developed directly from the Atlantic slave trade. Though realizing that is unsettling, next week we'll look in depth at that reality. Comprehending how this happened can, in turn, help us learn how racism can be overcome through the power of Christ that works within us. After all:

- Understanding the foundations of a lie can become the key to rejecting it and embracing truth.
- Since there is nothing innate about racism, we are in no way bound to perpetuate it.
- As believers, we are empowered and expected by Christ to stand against it.

JOURNAL

Take a moment to read this paraphrased version of Galatians 3:26–29 and circle the word *all* in every instance where Paul uses it. What do you suppose he is emphasizing through such repetition?

"So in Christ Jesus you are all children of God through faith, for all of you—no matter who you are or from where you've come—who were baptized into Christ have clothed yourselves with Christ.

"Whites are not better than Blacks, those with significant financial means are not better than those without them, nor is a man better than a woman; for you are all equally one in Christ Jesus.

"Indeed, if you belong to Christ, then you are all Abraham's seed, and equally heirs according to the promise."

In reflecting on some of the race and class divisions we typically face in the United States today, list two or three disparities in society that Paul's teaching in Galatians 3:28 can help us address. (An example is provided to get things started.)

1. It's unjust for women to be paid a lower wage than men who perform the exact same work since both men and women are equally human and created in the image of God.

2.

3.

4.

DAY 4
RELATIONSHIPS

As we have discussed, extreme differences of opinion and viewpoints exist even within the body of Christ. But from where do such differences arise? Without a doubt, one's ethnic and cultural heritage, gender, socio-economic status, and age all impact the way one lives and looks at life. Such things shape our worldview, which can be defined as the way we interpret reality as a whole and the specific things we experience. Our worldview, then, is the lens through which we look at and evaluate everything from today's news to a friend's new haircut!

When we embrace Christ by faith, we receive new life—eternal life, yes—but not necessarily a new worldview. This is an important truth to understand. Sure, the apostle Paul described believers as new creatures in Christ: The old has passed away, all things have become new (see 2 Cor. 5:17). In terms of worldview, however, this does not mean that our past experience or understanding of reality is without merit or value. What is new is how God uses our perspective and experience for spiritual and social good when we humbly allow him to do so. As Paul wrote to the church at Rome, "In all things God works for the good of those who love him, who have been called according to his purpose" (Rom. 8:28). This includes our past pain, personal experience, personalities, and preferences.

Therefore, in seeking to develop cross-cultural relationships with fellow members of a local church, it is important to keep in mind that your way is just *a* way of seeing things and not necessarily *the* way of seeing things. Of course, personal relationships are important to the health and well-being of any church. In a multiethnic church, however, they are of exponentially greater importance! Indeed, relationships form the very foundation and fabric of a multiethnic church because trust is not a commodity easily gained in an environment where people must interact with others different from themselves. And get this: cross-cultural relationships take much more time to form and develop. They cannot be agenda driven.

Now, we should recognize that all of us from time to time have prejudicial thoughts and feelings because of past conditioning from family, social settings, peer interactions, community mores, and the media. The question is, what should be done with prejudicial thoughts and feelings when they arise?

Before we delve into that question, which will happen in later discussions, an important point should be raised. The word *prejudice* can be defined as "a preformed opinion concerning someone or something." More often than not, the term is used to describe the negative or inaccurate opinions we have preformed of others with whom we have had (in most cases) little to no relational contact. However, some people have had legitimately negative encounters with others who are different from them, and these experiences have, quite naturally, shaped their thoughts and feelings.

Therefore, in attempting to encourage cross-cultural relationships, we should be careful not to denigrate those who share honestly about themselves in this regard. Rather, to build a healthy multiethnic church, we should provide opportunities for open dialogue and commend those with both the courage to discuss such things and the determination to deal with them. When misunderstandings arise, we must determine to stick it out.

JOURNAL

• • ● • •

Take a moment to consider your own past: For instance, where you were born, how you were raised, where you were educated, when you received Christ, and any other key things that shaped you as a person. Summarize them.

How did these aspects of your own past shape your present worldview?

COMMUNICATION

Our worldview causes communication to get complex, especially when we add a cross-cultural dimension. A person acts according her culture's values and norms, and the person interpreting those actions interprets them from his. For example, a White person taking a flight may assume that if his Black flight attendant is somehow inattentive, she fits a stereotype of a Black person with a chip on her shoulder. In fact, the flight attendant may have just received devastating news from home and be too upset to be as courteous as she would have been otherwise. Remaining conscious of our worldview, and understanding that others have their own as well, can help us exercise more patience and achieve more clarity in communicating cross-culturally with others.

In addition, we should:

1. Spend time getting to know the diverse people we are involved with at church, at school, or on the job, beyond just the work or the task at hand.

2. Listen to diverse others with the sincere goal of understanding their perspective.

3. When leading people of various ethnic or economic backgrounds, avoid undermining their authority (whether intentionally or unintentionally) if and when we have given them a specific role or responsibility.

Beyond these things, it can help to think of communication using this iceberg analogy[4]:

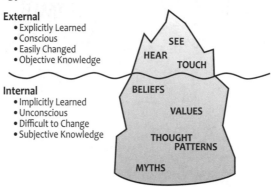

External
- Explicitly Learned
- Conscious
- Easily Changed
- Objective Knowledge

Internal
- Implicitly Learned
- Unconscious
- Difficult to Change
- Subjective Knowledge

SEE
HEAR
TOUCH

BELIEFS
VALUES
THOUGHT PATTERNS
MYTHS

In this illustration, all that we can see on the outside is external. In communication, this would include someone's words, tone, and body language or actions.

But all those things that can be perceived this way are based on our own beliefs, values, and thought patterns—that is, those things that form our worldview. And those kinds of internal things lie beneath the surface. Hidden away, they are understood implicitly, occur unconsciously, are difficult to change, and can only be known subjectively.

In cross-cultural communication, it's often the things that lie below the surface that differ dramatically enough to cause misunderstandings. For example, two different people may act the same way, yet be caused to do so by two very different things below the surface. A dinner guest removes his shoes upon entering the host's home. In the guest's culture, taking your shoes off is considered respectful to the host. Leaving them on would be rude. In the host's culture, this action is considered presumptuous, even disrespectful. In such a situation, without understanding each other, both parties could be hurt. Knowing what was below the surface made all the difference in understanding the action happening above the surface.

Without taking the time to explore what's below the surface in a person's life, we will find ourselves confused or frustrated at points. Confusion and frustration, if left unchecked, will lead to further misunderstandings and a breakdown of trust. Once this occurs, it's very hard to rebuild it.

With this in mind, keep short accounts with diverse others. Realize that what you assume lies behind someone else's words or actions may be wrong. Be willing to go to them time and time again, if necessary, to make sure you've heard them correctly, that they've heard you clearly, and that there's nothing outstanding between you.

JOURNAL

One way of avoiding misunderstanding in communication is to check your perceptions using the "drive-through" method. For instance, when you stop at a McDonald's and the cashier checks your order, he doesn't add value judgments such as, "Haven't you already had three strawberry shakes this week?" He simply repeats your order to make sure he has it correct.

Likewise, at the next available opportunity, repeat back to someone what you think you heard from him and ask, "Did I hear you correctly?" Once you're certain of what's been said, go on to explore what has been communicated by asking good questions and seeking further insights.

Spend time this week experimenting with the drive-through method.

Return here to record what you learned or experienced.

Take a moment to sketch what confusion and frustration looks like to you when two people are failing miserably at communication. Do not use words!

DAY 6
COMPETENCE

Earlier this week, we looked at historical examples of denominations that have fractured along ethnic lines and considered some of the ways in which cross-cultural communication, or a lack of diverse relationships, may contribute to internal misunderstandings and ultimately division within the larger church.

The proliferation of monoethnic churches can also be explained as a response to the specialized needs of the various cultures among us. For example, the African-American Protestant church has historically provided a refuge of sorts for its congregants. Being part of a Black-controlled institution provided dignity and affirmation in the midst of an otherwise White-dominated and often oppressive society. Seven major denominations make up the African-American Protestant church, and they include the National Baptist Convention, the African Methodist Episcopal Church, and the Church of God in Christ.

In *The Post-Black & Post-White Church*,[5] Efrem Smith detailed a number of gifts the Black church has contributed to the American church. These include the gift of participatory and celebratory preaching, the gift of a justice-oriented theology, and the gift of missional community engagement. Each of these gifts is rooted deep in the history of Africans in America and has contributed something unique to the church nationally.

Churches formed around ethnic affinity traditionally serve as places of belonging and are characterized by deep, family-like relationships. Though these churches differ greatly in service style based on the ethnic groups involved, they share in common the role of perpetuating a specific culture. For example, Korean churches:

- act as the social center and means of cultural identification for Koreans in America;
- serve an educational function by teaching American-born Koreans the Korean language, history, and culture; and
- help keep Korean nationalism alive.[6]

As multiethnic churches are formed, it is critical that they understand the reason why churches that are more ethnocentric are important to the communities they serve. With this knowledge in mind, multiethnic churches can become a "safe place" for all to express their own culture and to co-create with others a new way of doing church.

As they work toward this goal, multiethnic church pastors and congregants alike are learning to walk as one by:

1. Communicating a theology and philosophy of multiethnic ministry that inspires vision and ownership.

2. Including representatives from varying people groups in all tiers of leadership throughout the church.

3. Raising the level of cross-cultural intelligence among members.

4. Establishing a governance process and policies that fit the complex cultural makeup of the congregation.

JOURNAL

• • ● • •

What do you believe are the benefits and strengths of membership in a multiethnic church?

Does your church have a plan to address the growing diversity of our society and, more specifically, the increasing diversity of the community in which it exists or will soon be established?

Why might it be especially challenging for minorities to create multi-ethnic churches? What can be done to make this a more fulfilling transition?

DAY 7
REFLECTION

As you read the following verses, ask the Lord to speak to your heart through them, based on what you've been learning.

Soon the news reached the apostles and other brothers in Judea that Gentiles also were being converted! But when Peter arrived back in Jerusalem, the Jewish believers argued with him. "You fellowshiped with Gentiles and even ate with them," they accused.

Then Peter told them the whole story. "One day in Joppa," he said, "while I was praying, I saw a vision—a huge sheet, let down by its four corners from the sky. Inside the sheet were all sorts of animals, reptiles, and birds which we are not to eat. And I heard a voice say, 'Kill and eat whatever you wish.'

"'Never, Lord,' I replied. 'For I have never yet eaten anything forbidden by our Jewish laws!'

"But the voice came again, 'Don't say it isn't right when God declares it is!'

"This happened three times before the sheet and all it contained disappeared into heaven. Just then three men who had come to take me with them to Caesarea arrived at the house where I was staying! The Holy Spirit told me to go with them and not to worry about their being Gentiles! These six brothers here accompanied me, and we soon arrived at the home of the man who had sent the messengers. He told us how an angel had appeared to him and told him to send messengers to Joppa to find Simon Peter! 'He will tell you how you and all your household can be saved!' the angel had told him.

"Well, I began telling them the Good News, but just as I was getting started with my sermon, the Holy Spirit fell on them, just as he fell on us at the beginning! Then I thought of the Lord's words when he said, 'Yes, John baptized with water, but you shall be baptized with the Holy Spirit.' And since it was God who gave these Gentiles the same gift he gave us when we believed on the Lord Jesus Christ, who was I to argue?"

When the others heard this, all their objections were answered and they began praising God! "Yes," they said, "God has given to the Gentiles, too, the privilege of turning to him and receiving eternal life!" (Acts 11:1–18 TLB)

The disciples were called Christians first at Antioch (Acts 11:26).

JOURNAL

• • ● • •

Write a prayer inspired by the verses you just read.

WEEK 4

SYSTEMIC ISSUES

• • ● • •

THEOLOGY

Few things capture the attention like a good mystery. In Ephesians, the apostle Paul spoke of "the mystery made known to me by revelation" (Eph. 3:3). He then mentioned a previous letter he had written to the church in which he addressed his "insight into the mystery of Christ" (v. 4). According to Paul, understanding this mystery had not been granted to past generations but had only "now been revealed by the Spirit to God's holy apostles and prophets" (v. 5).

A common error is to assume that the mystery of which Paul was speaking concerns the gospel—the good news message of Christ's life, death, resurrection, and atonement for the repentant sinner.[1]

Yet, while certainly a mystery of its own, this was not the mystery Paul was talking about. In verse six, he wrote: "This mystery is that through the gospel the Gentiles are heirs together with Israel, members together of one body and sharers in the promise in Christ Jesus" (v. 6).

This verse represents the very apex of the book, the point from which the rest derives its context and meaning.[2] In fact, it represents the very substance of Paul's life and ministry! Paul was not describing himself here as a minister of the gospel, but a minister of the mystery of Christ. Notice, too, that he calls himself a minister of *this* gospel—that is, of the good news concerning the unity of Jews and Gentiles in the local church (v. 7).

Such an understanding is further supported by Paul's words near the end of his letter, at which time he asks the local church at Ephesus to "Pray also for me . . . so that I will fearlessly make known the mystery of the gospel, for which I am an ambassador in chains" (6:19–20).

In light of Paul's words in Ephesians 3, it's appropriate to recall why his imprisonment began in Jerusalem. Acts 21:27–32 informs us that a mob had been incited by the false accusation that Paul had brought Gentiles into the "Jews Only" section of the temple. Later, in addressing the crowd, Paul offered a defense by telling his conversion story. Near the end of his remarks, he said something very interesting: "Then the Lord said to me, 'Go! I will send you far away to the Gentiles'" (Acts 22:21).

Now notice the next verse, the crowd's immediate response:

"The crowd listened to Paul until he said this. Then they raised their voices and shouted, 'Rid the earth of him! He's not fit to live!'" (Acts 22:22).

In other words, the Jewish crowd listened to Paul up until this statement, when he spoke of his calling to the Gentiles, implying Gentile inclusion in the local church and coming kingdom of God. It was only then, as Paul declared the "mystery of Christ," that he became its ambassador in chains (Eph. 6:20).

JOURNAL

• • ● • •

Take a moment to underline the word *mystery* each time it appears in the following passage:

Surely you have heard about the administration of God's grace that was given to me for you, that is, the mystery made known to me by revelation, as I have already written briefly. In reading this, then, you will be able to understand my insight into the mystery of Christ, which was not made known to people in other generations as it has now been revealed by the Spirit to God's holy apostles and prophets.

This mystery is that through the gospel the Gentiles are heirs together with Israel, members together of one body, and sharers together in the promise in Christ Jesus. (Eph. 3:2–6)

In the space below, complete each statement to highlight your understanding of the mystery as explained by Paul in Ephesians 3:2–6.

1. It is a mystery made

2. It is a mystery previously

3. It is a mystery of Christ not

4. It is a mystery that has now been

5. The mystery is

HISTORY

Last week we learned that the beginning of modern-era racism in America could be traced to the start of the Atlantic slave trade. But what was it about that particular slave trade that cultivated racism? After all, slavery had already existed for centuries before the birth of Christ.

In November 1620, a group of Christians signed the Mayflower Compact, thanking God for their New Jerusalem. Because the Puritans believed that they had received a mandate from God, they were completely dedicated to building a nation free of oppression and tyranny. Their passion and persistence resulted in game-changing ways of thinking about government that ultimately produced the Declaration of Independence and the United States Constitution. Nevertheless, their fervor for a new world order ironically also became the underlying justification for racism and slavery in that very same land.

When Africans were first brought to America in 1619, some, like any other indentured servants, worked for three to seven years and were then released from service.[3] Within twenty to thirty years (one generation), however, this changed. As the South's economy became more agrarian, landowners began to feel the need for a continuous labor source. And since Africans could not leave or blend in to the broader population like Whites or Native Americans, they became the ideal choice for generations of forced servitude.

Because the need for labor was tied to building a nation, considered a mission from God, using Africans as slaves became viewed as patriotic—even godly. For example, George Whitefield, the initiator of the Great Awakening, believed that, "the colonies could not succeed without unpaid slave labor and he could not alter that reality." He, himself, purchased a South Carolina plantation and owned seventy-five slaves.[4]

Another church leader of the day, Rev. W. M. Rogers, declared, "When a slave asks me to stand between him and his master, what does he ask? He asks me to murder a nation's life; and I will not do it, because I have a conscience, because there is a God."[5] In this quote, too, we see that the life and development of the country, not long after the nation's founding, was foremost in the minds of those in authority and power. Even in time, as pastors began to see slavery as an evil, many still weighed it against impeding America's progress and saw the latter as a greater evil.

Slavery was thus an economic arrangement; the vast expanses of America would have been useless without sufficient labor to exploit them.[6] African Americans filled this need in a major way. They also grew in number. By the time of the Civil War, African Americans made up 40 percent of the South's population.[7]

Ultimately, modern-era racism developed as a justification for slavery in the United States. And people believed, or came to believe, that this arrangement was actually better for the Africans. Statements such as, "Darkies are happier being slaves," or "Colored people are more like children than adults," were repeated and became part of the nation's culture. In fact, according to Michael O. Emerson and Christian Smith, "Such stereotypes had become so pervasive they were simply seen as God-created truths by most whites and many others."[8]

JOURNAL

• • ● • •

How might the development of America have been different without slave labor?

In light of what you've just read, explain why you think African Americans may not wholeheartedly agree with the statement, "America is a Christian nation."

DAY 3

CONSIDERATIONS

Sometimes people think that with the amount of time that has passed since slavery ended, life opportunities should have evened out by now. Unfortunately, the impact of slavery does not simply fade away with time. Another of its continuing legacies, beyond modern-day racism, is that America has become a racialized society. A racialized society is one in which "race matters profoundly for differences in life experiences, life opportunities, and social relationships. As a result, rewards are allocated unequally by racial group."[9] In the United States, for example, outcomes differ significantly by race in areas such as health, self-esteem, interest rates, and wealth.

One of the starkest examples of this reality can be seen in the following table that reflects median differences in income by educational level.

As you can see, at each educational level, the expected income for Whites is significantly higher than for all other races. On average, a non-White person would need to earn a graduate or professional degree in order to earn income equal to a White person with a bachelor's degree. For minorities, it can be discouraging to know that achievement is not equally valued in the marketplace.

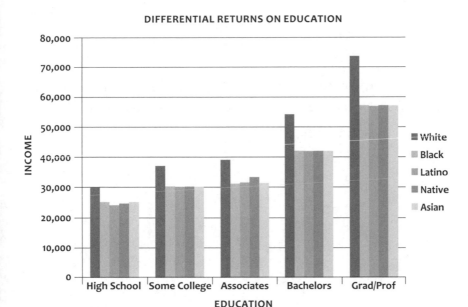

DIFFERENTIAL RETURNS ON EDUCATION

Even more detrimental than income disparity may be the perpetuation of racial stereotypes that hinder academic achievement in the first place.

To study the impact of racial stereotypes on performance, researchers gave Black and White study participants the task of putting on a ten-hole golf course. When told that the task measured their "sports psychology," Black and White participants performed equally. However, when told that the test measured their "natural athletic ability," White participants performed significantly worse than Black participants. And when told that the task measured "sports intelligence," the Black participants performed worse than both the White participants and the Black participants in the "sports psychology" group. When considering this, it's key to note that because of racial stereotypes, Black people have long been told by society that they are less intelligent, and that impacts how they view themselves. Likewise, Whites have been told they are less athletic. So going back to the study, we see that the mere presence of racial stereotypes subconsciously impacts their performance.[10] Think of the impact of this, for example, on a young, White athlete who dreams of being an NFL running back, or a Black student taking the SAT!

JOURNAL

∙ ∙ ● ∙ ∙

Name a few of the stereotypes that exist concerning your own racial group. Do these reflect negative or positive views of your culture?

How might these stereotypes have impacted your life to this point? How have they made you feel about yourself, your peers, and society in general?

RELATIONSHIPS

When considering the history and legacy of slavery, it's easy to understand why White and Black Christians may hold divergent views on a variety of issues today. In part, these views derive from each group having different experiences in and with the United States.

Within slavery specifically, "Blacks found a corporate identity in the biblical image of God's favored captives."[11] Therefore they naturally emphasized God's faithfulness to all those in captivity. Also with this corporate identity in mind, they did not reveal each other's sin, as to do so would damage the brotherhood. Even more so, informing against a fellow slave was strictly forbidden. "This responsibility to and for each other's safety was seen precisely as a *religious* duty."[12] Thus a more collectivist mind-set and tendencies within the African-American culture developed, in contrast to the rugged individualism of White Americans.

By definition, a collectivist puts the group's needs before the individual's needs and finds identity within the group. Therefore, African-American collectivism arose from the way African Americans were forced as one people into slavery and persisted even after emancipation, as they continued to be racially degraded throughout the dark years of segregation. Looking at life from the perspective of the group became, in many ways, essential to their survival. Life experience continues to validate this view as African Americans more often than not have been described as Black first: whether as Black teachers, Black inventors, Black farmers, or as a Black president, the racial descriptive is an inescapable part of African-American life.

By contrast, as a group, Whites have developed more individualistically than Blacks have in this country, gaining an individualism nourished in the soil of puritanical freedom. From the beginning, Whites have been largely afforded the ability to make choices as individuals rather than as part of a group. Their relationships with Christ, financial success or failure, and personal life outcomes have all (more often than not) been framed in the context of individual decisions and personal relationships.[13] Therefore, problems that Whites encounter in society are blamed on the individual's wrong choices, and the role of the group is minimized.

It is interesting, though not surprising, to learn how White and Black Americans have been broadly shaped by differences in their history in and with America. Such history provides us with perspective as we pursue a multiethnic Christian life. It helps us better understand what may lie beneath the surface in our interaction with diverse others. This is especially helpful when we find it difficult to communicate cross-culturally with one another.

JOURNAL

● ● ● ● ●

What principles might guide a collectivist? Are any of these principles biblical? If so, which ones?

What principles might guide an individualist? Are any of these principles biblical? If so, which ones?

COMMUNICATION

The way we think and perceive ourselves, whether as collectivists or individualists, profoundly impacts the way we communicate with each other cross-culturally. Consider the following letter, printed in *Christianity Today*, as a case in point:

Dear White Person:

Although we have known each other for centuries, we have not truly known each other. I, the black person, feel I know more about you because I had to [in order to make it in this country]. My will to survive forced me to learn about you. I was forced to learn your ways of doing things, forced to accept your concepts and values, and yet denied the right to share them. . . . If I tell you that I have hostility and anger within me, how do you interpret those emotions? Do they make me a savage who will riot and burn your property? . . . It seems to me that our society is presently paying for the many years of wrongs done to the black person. . . . In my rational moments, I can understand that you are the product of your forefathers' teachings, and are not entirely to blame for your feelings towards me. But if you or I should pass feelings of racial hatred on to our children, we stand condemned before God. . . . Along with my feelings of anger and hostility, there is a strong sense of disappointment. This disappointment is felt most keenly towards those who had taught me of God's love for all mankind. . . . I am still forbidden to attend some of your evangelical colleges and churches, and to be your neighbor. . . . I have been referring to myself as the black person. But I still feel I have not been allowed to reach compete adulthood. You have made me doubt my ability to compete with you intellectually, and you keep stunting this area of my life with inferior school systems. . . . I, the black person, suggest that you really get to know yourself. Evaluate your life experiences and see how they may have given you your views of the black person. . . . If that happens, it will enable us to love and to live together and enjoy the blessing God intended us to share.

Your fellow human being and future friend,
The Black Person[15]

JOURNAL

• • ● • •

Although this letter was written more than forty years ago, the author's emotion still resonates today. What did you think and feel when you read the letter?

Look back at the author's statement, "I, the black person, feel I know more about you because I had to [in order to make it in this country]." Do you think that some people still find truth in these words? In other words, do you feel that there is a normative way of doing things in America, and, if so, whose culture does it most fit or represent? Explain your answer.

COMPETENCE

In a subsequent issue of *Christianity Today*, a response to the letter from the Black Person was published. It read:

Dear Black Person:

Thank you for your wonderful letter. . . . I cannot claim to speak for the whole white race as I write this letter. Although I am sure that many others feel as I do, I can only speak for myself. For many years I was guilty of ignorance. . . . I did not know that black men were routinely but rudely questioned just for walking along the street, or that black homes were frequently invaded without benefit of warrant. Things like that never got in the news that reached me. . . . I am guilty. I admit my guilt. But more importantly, I have repented. I have sought forgiveness of the Christ-Savior of white and black and every person, and I am seeking to educate myself and others so that the gap of racial misunderstanding and abuse may yet be closed. . . . I was especially touched by this statement in your letter: "I am telling you these things because I want you to know me." I feel the same way about you: I am telling you these things because I want you to know me. . . . I want you to know that in order to raise my level of awareness I have been sitting at the feet of black authors like . . . William Pannell and Tom Skinner. . . . I realize that [white] evangelicals are not the only offenders. . . . But we are offenders, God help us. God forgive us. And please, Black Person, give us your forgiveness too. . . . [T]he important goal to strive for in all my relationships is caring for other individuals as individuals . . . please judge me not by my color but by my individual spirit. . . . And please, when I reach out my hand in friendship to you, take it.

Your fellow human being,
A White Person[16]

JOURNAL

• • ● • •

Consider both of the letters you've read. Notice the differences between them in terms of communication styles and patterns:

- The Black writer used a personal letter to speak from "one race to another." This is an example of someone writing from a more collectivist point of view. He brings up issues of relationship between two groups, Black and White, and looks for broad community understanding to bring about solutions and change.
- The White writer writes from an individualistic point of view stating, "I can only speak for myself." Looking only to herself and to her own personal efforts and responsibilities at outreach to improve race relations within her own sphere of influence, she seems, to a collectivist, not to have any vision for impact outside that sphere, or the need for vital systemic change.

Despite both authors having written heartfelt, sincere letters seeking understanding and reconciliation, how do the unintentional differences make it harder for these two Christians to fully appreciate or understand one another as they work toward their goal?

Based on the content of the second letter, how do you think its author felt in reading the Black person's message?

How do you think the author of the first letter might have felt in reading the White person's response?

REFLECTION

As you read the following verses, ask the Lord to speak to your heart through them, based on what you've been learning.

Now to him who is able to establish you in accordance with my gospel, and the message I proclaim about Jesus Christ, in keeping with the revelation of the mystery hidden for long ages past, but now revealed and made known through the prophetic writings by the command of the eternal God, so that all the Gentiles might come to the obedience that comes from faith—to the only wise God be glory forever through Jesus Christ! Amen. (Rom. 16:25–27)

Pray on my behalf, that utterance may be given to me in the opening of my mouth, to make known with boldness the mystery of the gospel, for which I am an ambassador in chains; that in *proclaiming* it I may speak boldly, as I ought to speak. (Eph. 6:19–20 NASB)

JOURNAL

• • ● • •

Write a prayer inspired by the verses you just read.

WEEK 5

WHAT GOD IS DOING

THEOLOGY

Many people familiar with the Bible refer to 1 Corinthians 13 as "the love chapter." However, when considering the placement of the apostle Paul's timeless treatise, have you ever asked yourself, "Why here, why now?" In other words, what's its purpose, and why is this chapter sandwiched between chapters twelve and fourteen, which discuss the use and nature of spiritual gifts within the local church?

Paul wrote chapter thirteen to show his readers "the most excellent way" to be one in the church for the sake of the gospel (compare 1 Cor. 12:31 with 12:12–13).[1] We are to manifest and model authentic love for one another in and through the local church beyond race or class distinctions (compare 12:12–13 with 13:13). In other words, loving one another beyond the superficial divisions of this world is the most powerful way to express the reality, presence, and blessing of God's love before a lost and dying world.

Therefore, Paul wanted us to understand that the way of love is much more than a feeling. It's a path to follow; a mind-set for the church to embrace (14:1). Indeed, we are to express genuine love for every member of the body, even the ones who seem "unpresentable" to us (12:23), or who, at times, stretch us beyond the limits of our own personalities and preferences.

Closer examination of the text reveals that 1 Corinthians 12–14 mirrors Ephesians 3–4, a passage in which the apostle Paul urged members of another multiethnic church—at Ephesus—"to live a life worthy of the calling [to be one in Christ and in the church] you have received" (Eph. 4:1–3). Keep in mind that in both cases, the same man wrote the same message of faith, hope, and love to diverse believers learning to walk, work, and worship God together as one in the local church. Through the unity of diverse believers pursuing Christ as one body, one new man, and one holy temple in which God is pleased to dwell (Eph. 2:14–22), the world will see an authentic expression of God's love for all people and believe (John 17:23).

So . . . faith, hope and love. But why is love the greatest of these? (1 Cor. 13:13).

Love is eternal. Think about it. In heaven there will be no need for faith or hope. Faith and hope are things we exercise on earth. God, however, is and will forever be love. Therefore, Paul would have us express eternal, unconditional love to one another on earth as it is in heaven, beyond race or class distinctions, for the sake of the gospel. Yes, it is love that forms the foundation of a healthy multiethnic church, and love that is required to live a multiethnic Christian life.

JOURNAL

• • ● • •

Read the following list of verses and the truths they share about the body of Christ.[2] Approach this with a prayerful heart for what God may want to say to you through them. Make a note of what he tells you.

UNITY OF THE BODY

1 Corinthians 12:12–27

- We should be one Spirit and one body, whether Jews or Greeks (see v. 13).
- There should be no division in the body (v. 25).
- The parts (of the body) should have equal concern for each other (see v. 25).

Ephesians 4:3–6, 16

- Make every effort to keep the unity (v. 3).
- There is one body and one Spirit (v. 4).
- The whole body must be joined and held together by every supporting ligament (see v. 16).

GIFTS OF THE BODY

1 Corinthians 12:28–30; 14:2

- God gives various ministries and gifts: apostles, prophets, teachers . . . and gifts of healing, helping, administration, and more (see 12:28).

Ephesians 4:7, 11–13

- God appoints some as apostles, prophets, evangelists, pastors, and teachers (see v. 11).

CORRECTION OF THE BODY

1 Corinthians 12:25 — 14

- In your immaturity, you are seeking showy gifts.
- Avoid divisions; seek love above all (see 12:25, 29–31).

Ephesians 4:14–16

- No prolonged infancies among us, please (see v. 14).
- Mature as one in love (see v. 15).

LOVE IN THE BODY

1 Corinthians 13

- If I speak but have not love, nothing else matters (see v. 1).
- Love is patient, love is kind. . . . It is not rude, not self-seeking (see vv. 4–5).

Ephesians 4:2, 15–16

- Be patient, bearing with one another in love (v. 2).
- Speak the truth in love (see v. 15).

BUILDING UP THE BODY

1 Corinthians 14:4–5, 12, 17, 19

- To edify, build up the church (see vv. 4–5, 12).

Ephesians 4:12

- Christ gave gifts so that the body of Christ may be built up (see v. 12).

MATURITY IN THE BODY

1 Corinthians 14:20

- Brothers and sisters, stop thinking like children (see v. 20).

Ephesians 4:13–14

- When we all become mature, we will no longer be infants (see v. 14).

HISTORY

From the desk of Dr. Michael O. Emerson, provost of North Park University in Chicago, Illinois, and professor of sociology, specializing in urban, race, and ethnic relations:

In 1998 a national study of American congregations found that just 5 percent of Protestant churches were racially diverse (in which no one ethnic group comprises more than 80 percent of attending members). At the time, no differences existed between large churches (one thousand or more attenders) and other churches.

When this same study was conducted in 2007, a major change was revealed: large Protestant churches were three times more likely to be multiethnic in 2007 than in 1998. And in narrowing considerations to evangelical churches, large congregations were five times more likely in 2007 than in 1998 to be multiethnic.

This is seismic change in such a short time. These changes have come about due to a spiritual movement that has emerged. Large churches typically are the bellwether of change to come throughout Christendom. More change, then, is coming. An old system is crumbling and a new one, the multiethnic congregation, is emerging.[3]

Take a look at what the trend Dr. Emerson mentioned actually looks like. The following chart shows the past and projected development of multiethnic churches in the United States.[4]

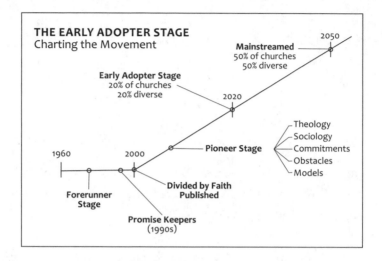

JOURNAL

• • ● • •

What do you believe are some of the reasons for the growing interest in building healthy multiethnic churches?

What does this growing interest say about the times in which we live, the people of God we are striving to become, the nature of the church, and the hope of the gospel?

DAY 3
CONSIDERATIONS

Recent studies reveal even more positive news regarding diversity in the church and confirm Dr. Emerson's observations, shared in the last chapter. Research from the 2010 *Faith Communities Today Survey* showed racial diversity continuing to increase in congregations throughout the United States.[5] As Dr. Scott Thumma pointed out in an article in the *Huffington Post*, the percentage of multiethnic congregations (using the 20 percent or more minority criteria) has nearly doubled in the past decade to 13.7 percent.[6]

More specifically, Thumma noted, "In 2010, 12.5 percent of all Protestant Christian churches and 27.1 percent of other Christian churches (Catholic/Orthodox) were multiracial. Multiracial Mainline Protestant churches accounted for 7.4 percent of their total, while 14.4 percent of Evangelical Protestant congregations were multiracial."[7]

Concerning the movement of American Christianity toward racial reconciliation in the 1990s, author Chris Rice wrote the following profound words: "Yes, deep reconciliation will produce justice and new relationships between the races. Yes, this will lead Christians to become a bright light of hope in the public square. But I have become convinced that God is not very interested in the church healing the race problem. I believe it is more true that God is using race to heal the church."[8]

JOURNAL

• • ● • •

Describe the ways in which your church and the churches in your area are reflecting, or are not yet reflecting, the statistics above. Why might this be true for your church or region?

How do you believe that God might be using racial diversity in these days to heal the church?

Ethiopia and Eritrea have been locked in national conflict since 1962, when Ethiopia annexed Eritrea. For thirty years, the two regions fought until Eritrea passed a referendum for independence in 1993. However, this meant Ethiopia lost access to the Red Sea and had to rely on Eritrea, or other countries, to import and export goods.

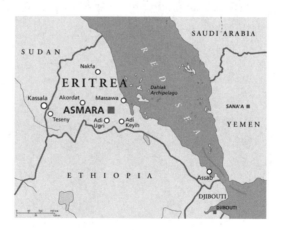

Following the referendum, and for a short time after, the two countries got along well. However, relations began to dissolve again in 1997 when Eritrea introduced its own currency. Soon after, in 1998, a border dispute between the two countries arose and led yet again to war. This war, lasting from May 1998 until June of 2000, resulted in one hundred thousand deaths and millions of dollars in economic loss. To this day, serious tensions remain between the two nations over disputed territories, often erupting in outbreaks of violence.

The bitter dispute between the two countries has created lasting enmity between Ethiopians and Eritreans. However, in the Habasha Fellowship at Peoples Church of Cincinnati, Ohio, people from these two nations worship God together as one. More than that, they support each other. They have come to realize that their bond in Christ is stronger than national alliances.

The ability of the Habasha Fellowship to genuinely care for one another has provided a testimony to families back in their homelands and to other Ethiopians and Eritreans in Cincinnati. This is the kind of testimony that every multiethnic church can provide, as each becomes a place where even the deepest divides are washed away by the blood of Jesus (Eph. 2:13). When we come together as one under the banner of Christ and without other distinctions, then families, friends, and entire cities will recognize the Prince of Peace who dwells among us. They will see our unity through faith in Jesus Christ overwhelms any historical divisions that otherwise keep us apart. As a result, many will come to know him as we do.

JOURNAL

Are there two or three nations or ethnic people groups you know of that have had historical conflict? Do these nations or groups remain in conflict today? Spend a moment in prayer for Christians within these groups, asking God to help them build bridges of faith, hope, and love across historic divisions.

In light of Ephesians 2:11–22, what should we expect of ourselves, and our local churches, in building cross-cultural relationships for the sake of the gospel?

COMMUNICATION

Perhaps you've said or heard others say, "If we'd just stop talking about racial issues, they would go away!" Sadly, this has proven not to be the case, either in the local church or in society as a whole. The fact is, without productive conversation about matters of race, there can be little change. No wonder, then, the percentage of churches throughout the United States that could authentically claim to be multiethnic remained fixed (at less than 10 percent) for well over one hundred years!

By contrast, over the past ten years, as the biblical mandate for the multiethnic church has been proclaimed, core commitments have been determined; objections and obstacles have been overcome in the local churches pursuing the vision; and the truth of such things has been widely disseminated so as to be embraced by church leaders. Finally, there is significant movement! This proves that the more we pursue the multiethnic Christian life, the more we will see God working in and through us in the local church to make it happen.

We can pursue such ends by:

- Openly discussing matters of race and ethnic divides.
- Respectfully engaging in difficult conversations about race.
- Pursuing cross-cultural relationships, communication, and competence.

As Scott Williams, author of *Church Diversity: Sunday, the Most Segregated Day of the Week,* has said, "The only way race will ever become a non-issue is if you make race an issue. You must confront the elephant in the pew."[9]

In recent years, many denominations and organizations have taken steps to move beyond segregation and position the American church for a more inclusive, multiethnic future. For example, in the 1990s, Promise Keepers held large rallies that in part called godly men to racial healing and reconciliation.[10] Another step was taken when denominations including the Southern Baptists and Assemblies of God in 1995, and the Episcopalians in 2000, made sweeping apologies for past racism in their ranks. More recently, the United Methodist Church took a step in April 2012, when the predominantly White denomination entered into a full communion agreement with five historically Black denominations. The leaders of these denominations agreed to recognize each other's churches as part of their organizational brotherhood, share sacraments, and affirm their clergy and ministries. None of this progress happened accidentally or by ignoring thorny matters of race. Each step was widely communicated and intentional.

As we pursue the multiethnic Christian life, we progress not by hiding our understanding of the gospel in regard to its call for unity, but by proclaiming it intentionally. We do so by expecting that our own local churches will reflect the kingdom of God, on earth as it is in heaven, and be filled with men and women from varying nations, tribes, and tongues, expressing their love for him, for one another, and for all those who do not yet know him as we do.

JOURNAL

• • ● • •

Can you think of any conflict that you might have, or have had, with a friend or family member that has not been discussed or remains unresolved? Has the conflict gotten better or worse over the years? What step might you take toward reconciliation?

What is one thing you are learning through this study that you might be willing to share within your circle of influence or with local church leaders?

COMPETENCE

"Are you so foolish? After beginning by means of the Spirit, are you now trying to finish by means of the flesh?" (Gal. 3:3).

Reading about other cultures, listening to others who are different from us, and building diverse relationships are all critical to pursuing cross-cultural competence. But at this point it's important to remember the one who is indispensable in the acquisition of such competence: namely, the Holy Spirit. He is the one who leads us into all truth. Without him we cannot live the multiethnic Christian life or hope to build healthy multiethnic churches.

From the moment of the Holy Spirit's arrival in Acts 2—the very beginning of the local church in Jerusalem—he began to break down barriers between people. Because he gave new believers the gift of tongues, linguistic obstacles were overcome as both Hebrew-speaking (Hebraic) and Greek-speaking (Hellenistic) Jews came together for teaching, fellowship, the breaking of bread, and prayer (Acts 2:42–47). Nevertheless, this alone did not prevent differences in culture from causing hurt and confusion in the emerging church, as seen in this passage: "In those days when the number of disciples was increasing, the Hellenistic Jews among them complained against the Hebraic Jews because their [the Hellenistic] widows were being overlooked in the daily distribution of food" (Acts 6:1).

The disciples solved this problem by exercising a great deal of cross-cultural competence. Luke, the author of Acts, described, "They chose

Stephen, a man full of faith and of the Holy Spirit; also Philip, Procorus, Nicanor, Timon, Parmenas, and Nicolas from Antioch, a convert to Judaism," to be deacons and oversee the food distribution (Acts 6:5). The names of these men indicate that each of them was Hellenistic! In other words, Luke said the Jewish leadership dealt with this cultural division by legitimizing the concerns of the minority people group and empowering minority leadership to ensure that their widows would not be overlooked in the future.

This paints a beautiful picture of the Holy Spirit working in his people cross-culturally and of church leadership promoting an inclusive spirit. The Holy Spirit not only brought these men together, but also gave them the wisdom and humility to solve a problem that threatened church unity.

Through the disciples we also see how the flesh and human nature can get in the way of our multiethnic efforts. For instance, Peter (also called Cephas) gave in to societal pressure and, more specifically, the religious expectations of the Jews in his day, by ceasing to eat with Gentile believers (Gal. 2:11–12). This led Paul to confront Peter publically in order to bring him back "in line with the truth of the gospel" (Gal. 2:14).

As we pursue the multiethnic Christian life, we will need to yield to the Holy Spirit and continually rely upon him to avoid confusion or discouragement. We will need his wisdom to address any challenges as we proceed. And we will need him to keep our hearts purposed in this direction and mindful that being one with diverse others in the local church is biblical and essential to being filled up "to the measure of all the fullness of God" (Eph. 3:14–21). Even when it seems easier to be part of a homogeneous church that more comfortably matches our personal preferences, the Holy Spirit empowers us to live in the supernatural by reminding us that it's not about us — it's all about him. Indeed, he is what keeps us walking, working, and worshiping God together as one in Christ and in the church for the sake of the gospel.

JOURNAL

• • ● • •

"So I say, walk by the Spirit, and you will not gratify the desires of the flesh. For the flesh desires what is contrary to the Spirit, and the Spirit what is contrary to the flesh. . . . The fruit of the Spirit is love, joy, peace, forbearance, kindness, goodness, faithfulness, gentleness and self-control" (Gal. 5:16–17, 22–23).

Pick out one of the fruit of the Spirit listed in this passage and describe how it might help you in pursuit of cross-cultural competence.

How might your own personal preferences get in the way of pursuing a multiethnic Christian life?

REFLECTION

As you read the following verses, ask the Lord to speak to your heart through them, based on what you've been learning.

For he himself is our peace, who has made the two groups one and has destroyed the barrier, the dividing wall of hostility, by setting aside in his flesh the law with its commands and regulations. His purpose was to create in himself one new humanity out of the two, thus making peace, and in one body to reconcile both of them to God through the cross, by which he put to death their hostility. He came and preached peace to you who were far away and peace to those who were near. For through him we both have access to the Father by one Spirit.

Consequently, you are no longer foreigners and strangers, but fellow citizens with God's people and also members of his household, built on the foundation of the apostles and prophets, with Christ Jesus himself as the chief cornerstone. In him the whole building is joined together and rises to become a holy temple in the Lord. And in him you too are being built together to become a dwelling in which God lives by his Spirit. (Eph. 2:14–22)

JOURNAL

• • ● • •

Write a prayer inspired by the verses you just read.

WEEK 6

HOW SHOULD I RESPOND?

• • ● • •

THEOLOGY

In Ephesians 4, Paul turned his attention to practical Christian living. But what often goes unnoticed is that he did so with the multiethnic nature of the church in mind. A way to understand this is to ask a question prompted by Ephesians 4:1: What was the calling in which the Ephesians were called to walk worthily? Contextually, it was the call for Jewish converts and Gentile believers to love one another and to walk, work, and worship God together as one in and through the local church for the sake of the gospel. It remains a calling for us and for the local church today. But how, practically, can we achieve this?

To answer this, Paul instructed the diverse believers at Ephesus to walk together in "humility and gentleness, with patience, showing tolerance for one another in love, being diligent to preserve the unity of the Spirit in the bond of peace" (Eph. 4:2–3 NASB). Here he outlined the values and attitudes required of everyone who would pursue a multiethnic Christian life.

Experience tells us that it's much easier to walk humbly, be gentle, show forbearance, and love others with whom we share the same ethnic, educational, or economic background, than it is to walk with those who are different from us. Therefore, unity and diversity cannot otherwise be achieved apart from the willingness of everyone involved to embrace these attitudes. This is why the vast majority of local churches today remain segregated. People naturally gravitate to what is most comfortable—but that doesn't mean we should.

Consider the lives of Christ, the apostles, and other heroes of our faith. Rarely will you find any of them living comfortably. In fact, they wholeheartedly abandoned themselves to God's will by sacrificing their own preferences for a greater good. The question is: Are we in the twenty-first century willing to leave behind what is otherwise easy, natural, and comfortable, in order to walk, work, and worship God in unity with diverse individuals for the sake of the gospel?[2]

- Only in so doing will "the manifold wisdom of God . . . be made known through the church" (Eph. 3:10 NASB).
- Only in so doing will we "be able to comprehend with all the saints what is the breadth and length and height and depth, and to know the love of Christ which surpasses knowledge" (vv. 18–19 NASB).
- Only in so doing will we see God do "far more abundantly beyond all that we ask or think, according to the power that works within us" (v. 20 NASB).

JOURNAL

∙ ∙ ● ∙ ∙

How do you define humility?

What does walking humbly with others look like practically?

Why do you think men and women naturally gravitate to what's comfortable?

Who is someone you know or know of who sacrificed his or her own personal preferences for the greater good in order to advance God's will and agenda? What character qualities does his or her life exhibit?

HISTORY

At first glance, the opening portion of one of the Bible's most perplexing books may seem a surprising place to find clear insights into life as a multiethnic church. Peek into the history behind the writing, however, and one discovers shades of meaning that bring the truths to light.

The apostle John wrote the book of Revelation and addressed it to seven churches in Asia (Rev. 1:4). In it, John shared Christ's message to each specific church. Beginning in chapter 2 with the church at Ephesus, Christ commended the congregation first for its (good) deeds, toil, and perseverance. Describing the church as steadfast, he noted they had endured the widespread persecution that believers faced during this time. However, in the very next verse, Christ chastised the church, saying "But I have this against you . . . you have left your first love" (Rev. 2:4). The question is: What was this "first love"?

Throughout the years, most believers have been taught that the first love is a love for Christ or, more specifically, a passionate relationship with him. In this sense, the word first has to do with priority, nature, or quality. While a worthwhile point that highlights key scriptural truths taught elsewhere, this particular Scripture speaks to something else. The phrase is more correctly translated from the Greek, "the love that you had at first," as clarified in Revelation 2:5. In other words, the question of first love here is not so much a question of priority, but one of prior love.

In order to see what prior love the Ephesians had, look at Ephesians 1:15–16 (written many years earlier): "For this reason I too, having heard of the faith in the Lord Jesus which [exists] among you, and your love for all the saints, do not cease giving thanks for you, while making mention of you in my prayers" (NASB).

Here's the point: Within a generation or so of Paul's commendation for its faith and love, Christ rebukes the church at Ephesus for no longer loving all the saints as it did at the first, or in the beginning, whether they were of Jewish or Gentile descent.

Now notice how Revelation 2:2–5 parallels Ephesians 1:15:

- Both commend faith (compare Rev. 2:2–3 with Eph. 1:15).
- Both mention love (compare Rev. 2:4 with Eph. 1:15).

The only difference is that at the time Paul wrote, Jewish and Gentile converts in the church at Ephesus were expressing love for one another. A generation or so later, by the time of John's writing, they were not. Thus, Christ sternly rebuked the church: "Therefore remember from where you have fallen, and repent and do the deeds you did at first; or else I am coming to you and will remove your lampstand out of its place—unless you repent" (Rev. 2:5 NASB).

For far too long we have turned a blind eye to the lack of diversity within our congregations:

- We've proudly championed homogeneity in church planting by basing our plans on demographic targets or advocating the homogeneous unit principle.
- We've celebrated numeric growth and attendance more than community revitalization and transformation.
- We've encouraged the purchase of land and built new buildings instead of repurposing abandoned space in the community, thus providing a physical manifestation of the power and message of redemption.

- We've failed, often even refused, to empower minority leadership or to share authoritative responsibility with people of color.
- We've undermined our credibility by calling for unity and justice on social media from the otherwise segregated churches that we lead or attend.

JOURNAL

If Jesus were writing to the church you attend today, what thing(s) would he commend? If Jesus were writing to the church you attend today, what thing(s) would he condemn?

Do you believe the church in America is in danger of having its lampstand removed due to the systemic segregation of the local church and our collective failure to love all the saints, without distinction or division, as we have been otherwise called to do? What evidence or experience can you provide to support your belief one way or the other?

CONSIDERATIONS

The reality that a majority of local churches today remain segregated by race and class significantly impacts our society. For instance, despite similar religious views, White and Black evangelicals differ dramatically in their political opinions and voting habits. Interestingly, their perspectives vary even more widely than the views of Black and White Americans who do not attend church.

This disparity can be readily observed in recent presidential elections:

- In 2004, 58 percent of White voters supported George W. Bush in contrast to the 11 percent of Black voters. More specifically, 78 percent of White evangelicals that year supported Bush, while 85 percent of Black evangelicals supported his challenger, John Kerry.[1]
- In 2008, over 70 percent of White evangelicals favored John McCain, compared to 54 percent of White voters overall, while over 95 percent of Black evangelicals supported Barack Obama.[2]
- In 2012, 95 percent of Black evangelicals supported Obama, while 80 percent of White evangelicals supported his challenger, Mitt Romney, compared to 60 percent of White voters overall.[3]

So why are Christ-followers more likely than nonbelievers to be separated by race when it comes to political ideology? Once again, it has to do with the way we interpret reality, whether as individuals or as a collective. And because most churches are homogeneous, individual and collectivist points of view on various issues shape our churches as well. Therefore, the sermons we hear, and the relationships we form at church, with people most like us, influence our political thinking. Not that most churches directly endorse political candidates or party platforms. They simply cultivate common worldviews.

Due to local church segregation, Christians of varying backgrounds are generally isolated from one another. The absence of genuine relationships to bring us together helps to explain the many differences of opinion we hold in various areas of life, such as politics. Where we should otherwise be united by faith, sadly it divides us.

Another way in which Sunday morning segregation impacts society is observed in the way Black and White people interpret the gaps between them. For instance, when asked why Black people generally have lower incomes and worse housing, White conservative Protestants chose reasons that pointed to individual responsibility:

- 52 percent cited Black culture;
- 48 percent cited lack of motivation;
- 29 percent cited history.

In contrast, when non-church-going Whites were asked the same question, only 40 percent selected individual-based explanations, while 58 percent cited a more structurally-based, collectivist cause: lack of access to education.[4]

Among Black evangelicals, however, the effect of religious affiliation was exactly opposite. Church-going Black Protestants were more likely than non-church-going Blacks to cite structurally based reasons for the economic gaps between Blacks and Whites.

Church-Going Black Protestants
- 31 percent cited a lack of motivation
- 72 percent cited discrimination

Non-Church-Going Black Protestants
- 42 percent cited lack of motivation
- 63 percent cited discrimination

It appears that conservative religion intensifies the varied values and experiences of each racial group, sharpening and increasing the divide between Black and White Americans.

The key to bridging these differences of opinion and becoming more like-minded is for Christians to develop cross-racial relationships. In fact, the same study showed a dramatic change in the opinions of White evangelicals who have African Americans in their relational networks. High-contact evangelicals were those who reported that an African-American lives in their neighborhood and that someone in their family has had an African American over for dinner in the past two years. Among this group, individualist and structurally-based (collectivist) causes for economic disparities by race were cited equally.[5]

JOURNAL

• • ● • •

Describe your own cross-cultural relationships in terms of high or low contact. Write the word *high* or *low* next to the ethnic groups (different from your own) listed below. Remember high contact means that someone from the group mentioned lives in your neighborhood and has come to your house for a meal in the past two years.

- Black   _____
- White   _____
- Asian   _____
- Hispanic   _____
- Other   _____ (which other group specifically)
    _____

Write down the names of one to three people from varying ethnic groups whom you know and with whom you would like to pursue a deepening relationship.

RELATIONSHIPS

As people pursue a multiethnic Christian life, and through involvement in a multiethnic church, cross-cultural relationships deepen along a continuum that Barron Witherspoon Sr., author of *The Fallacy of Affinity*, called the cross-culture worship model (CCW). The model describes relational movement along a continuum beginning with integration and maturing to reconciliation.

| Integration | Penetration | Reconciliation |

The continuum begins with simple integration, which Witherspoon described as "the conscious effort to bring different races into physical proximity for corporate worship and fellowship."[6] As relationships form, they progress from integration to what Witherspoon describes as penetration, whereby those involved gain "subsurface insight into the core values and felt needs of people from another racial heritage." Within this phase, "two Christians, from different cultural backgrounds, invest in each other's spiritual growth and well-being."[7] These relationships foster new knowledge and understanding of God from a different cultural perspective. In these relationships, iron sharpens iron even more so than it does within our own affinity group alone, as we increase the width and depth of personal and relational exchange.

Honest engagement, transparency, and trust in these cross-cultural relationships lead ultimately to reconciliation, which Witherspoon defined as "a state of Christian symbiosis characterized by high trust level, candid communication and shared leadership."[8]

Biblically speaking, reconciliation includes being reconciled to God as well as to our fellow man. Reconciliation is the Holy Spirit's work performed in our hearts as we pursue growth in Christ together as one in faith and one in the church. Reconciliation, however, is risky because it involves interdependence. Nevertheless, in the reconciliation phase we realize how much we enjoy each other personally beyond the worldly distinctions that otherwise divide. We also discover that we need each other in order to advance God's kingdom and provide a credible witness to the world of his love for all people.

Quite simply, God intends for us to live reconciled to one another on earth as we will live one day in heaven. Living in reconciliation is not only our destiny, but also a ministry to which we've been called here and now (see 2 Cor. 5:18).

JOURNAL

∘ ● ● ●

What are some of the challenges to building cross-cultural relationships with those who are not Christ-followers?

What are two to three steps that you believe must be taken to move a cross-cultural relationship through each of the phases of reconciliation as described in the CCW model?

From integration to penetration:

Step 1

Step 2

Step 3

From penetration to reconciliation:

Step 1

Step 2

Step 3

Why do so many cross-cultural interactions seemingly fail to reach the goal of reconciliation?

COMMUNICATION

Sometimes cross-cultural relationships fail to progress to the maturity of reconciliation because of a lack of communication skills. Early in this study, we discussed the drive-through method as one way of working on these skills. Another communication skill necessary to building cross-cultural relationships is what some call the Matthew 18:15 principle.

Specifically, Matthew 18:15 provides instruction on how to correct an individual within the church. However, the principle it teaches can also be useful in helping us overcome cross-cultural misunderstandings. Here's the text: "If your brother or sister sins, go and point out their fault, just between the two of you. If they listen to you, you have won them over."

In other words, the Matthew 18:15 principle tells us to go and talk directly with a person if we ever feel insulted or offended by something he or she says or does. This is a fundamentally important principle when seeking to build cross-cultural relationships and pursue cross-cultural competence with others in a multiethnic church. In fact, in a multiethnic church, there is a 100 percent chance of being offended at some point along the way! Keeping short accounts and giving others the benefit of the doubt goes a long way in developing cross-cultural relationships marked by transparency and trust, the bonds of which, once formed, are not easily broken.

Talking things out with others in such instances does not in and of itself lead to conflict resolution. At times, our efforts create even further confusion.

But don't let the fear of misunderstanding keep you from applying the Matthew 18:15 principle. More often than not, the other party will not realize what they have said or done and will be open to understanding just how and why their statement or action offended you. Even in rare situations when someone has insulted you on purpose, by applying this principle you open a door for him or her to apologize through your own kindness.

And one more thing: Help others exercise this principle by refusing to listen to them talk about others who have offended them. Rather, encourage direct communication with the one who caused the offense.

What if the other person takes what I say the wrong way and gets upset? Applying the Matthew 18:15 principle means direct confrontation; admittedly, for some, this is uncomfortable. To help avoid any escalating confusion or conflict, be sure to approach tricky communication using "I" statements instead of "you" statements. This means that you should tell the other person how you are feeling or how you heard something, instead of trying to tell them that what they did was wrong and why.

For example, in going to another person, you might ask or say:

- Help me understand . . .
- To be honest, I was confused (or hurt) by . . .
- Perhaps I misunderstood . . .
- Did I hear what was said correctly? Maybe I'm mistaken . . .

Another important cross-cultural communication strategy involves framing the conversation in a positive way so as to ensure that not all that is said (or heard) is negative.

With this goal in mind, think of a conversation as a sandwich. You begin with the bread of kindness. Start with a genuine compliment or share how important the relationship is to you. For example:

- You know, we've been friends for a long time, and I want you to know how special you are to me; or,

* I know we're just getting to know each other, but you've already taught me a lot.

Having framed the conversation in a non-threatening way, you can then add the meat of confrontation. Honestly and specifically share about what has offended you in a way that is designed to preserve the relationship. Speak the truth in love (see Eph. 4:15). And make sure you do not assume another's underlying motives. Keep the iceberg analogy seen on page 78 in mind. Remember to be just as willing to listen as you are to speak in order to get below the surface for clarity and healing.

Finally, close with the bread of peaceful parting. By opening and concluding the conversation with love and affirmation, you create the best chance for a productive conversation.

JOURNAL

▪ ● ● ● ▪

A friend at church has offended you by posting a politically controversial comment on Facebook and tagged you in the process. How should you respond?

Write three statements to frame your hypothetical response in a non-threatening way using the sandwich metaphor to foster a non-threatening and productive conversation.

Bread of Kindness:

Meat of Confrontation:

Bread of Peaceful Parting:

COMPETENCE

Developing cross-cultural relationships as part of a multiethnic church can actually help heal racial inequalities in our broader society. For instance, a recent article in the *Christian Post* described how multiethnic churches could help close the income gap between Whites and minorities. As one example, the author wrote, "Social networking influences the sharing of information that aids job advancement."[9] In this way, interacting across racial lines can help promote or advance career opportunities for everyone involved.

As you grow in understanding and practicing a multiethnic Christian life, you will also begin to notice, and think about, the neighborhood in which you live. Though less segregated than local churches, neighborhoods still tend to be concentrated by race or ethnicity in many parts of the country. This impacts what economists call "wealth acquisition."

The most typical means by which Americans gain wealth is through purchasing their homes and benefiting from the increasing value those properties can have. While home values in general took a substantial hit during the 2008 financial crisis, the impact has not proven to be equal across the board. On average, neighborhoods with a majority Black population saw a 28 percent greater decline in their housing values than did neighborhoods that were majority White.[10] This created a widening gap of wealth between Whites and others, particularly Blacks and Latinos.

Generally speaking, White Americans have eighteen times as much wealth as Latinos and twenty times as much wealth as African Americans in the average economy. These gaps, however, have increased rather than decreased over the past twenty years.[11]

Given the wealth gap, and its effect on neighborhood consolidation by race or ethnicity, there exists a higher chance that Black families will remain in overwhelmingly poor neighborhoods. Statistically, a Black family with income below the poverty level is twelve times more likely than a White family to live in a neighborhood in which at least 40 percent of the residents are poor. Beyond the sociological and psychological impact of being surrounded by poverty, this impacts opportunities for a quality education among minorities. Because schools are funded by local property taxes, resources are largely dictated by a neighborhood's wealth. Even when a White child lives in a poor neighborhood, that neighborhood likely has a lower concentration of poverty than others. Her school will receive more funding and enjoy greater resources. Thus her chances of attending a quality neighborhood school will be higher than a poor Black child living in or near a city's center.

In every area where we see the impact of racialization on society, believers who are willing to live a multiethnic Christian life bring the message of Christ and hope. Through our unity in faith and purpose, the effects of racialization start to lose their grip. Imagine if all of our churches and our neighborhoods looked more like heaven. Property values would be stable and equitable. Schools would provide an equal and quality education for every child. Stereotypes would fade. And everyone would be welcome at the dinner table.

In this scenario, unity is not an outcome of mere tolerance. It is forged through the bonds of godly, unconditional love that creates a much more peaceful society, fosters mutual respect across the races, encourages sharing of our lives and resources, and promotes equal opportunity for all people God created in his image and loves.

JOURNAL

· ● ● ● ·

What does your own neighborhood look like? What criteria did you use in choosing to live in this particular neighborhood? If not by choice, what factors dictated that you would live in this neighborhood?

How might a healthy multiethnic church impact an impoverished neighborhood or help with community development?

DAY 7

REFLECTION

As you read the following verses, ask the Lord to speak to your heart through them, based on what you've been learning.

Therefore if there is any encouragement in Christ, if there is any consolation of love, if there is any fellowship of the Spirit, if any affection and compassion, make my joy complete by being of the same mind, maintaining the same love, united in spirit, intent on one purpose. Do nothing from selfishness or empty conceit, but with humility of mind regard one another as more important than yourselves; do not merely look out for your own personal interests, but also for the interests of others. (Phil. 2:1–4 NASB)

Live a life worthy of the calling you have received. Be completely humble and gentle; be patient, bearing with one another in love. Make every effort to keep the unity of the Spirit through the bond of peace. There is one body and one Spirit, just as you were called to one hope when you were called; one Lord, one faith, one baptism; one God and Father of all [people], who is over all [people] and [working] through all [people] and in all [people]. (Eph. 4:1–6)

JOURNAL

• • ● • •

Write a prayer inspired by the verses you just read.

WEEK 7

HOW SHOULD
THE CHURCH RESPOND?

• • ● • •

THEOLOGY

One of the most intriguing things about the church at Antioch was the diversity of its leadership team. According to Acts 13:1, "In the church at Antioch there were prophets and teachers: Barnabas, Simeon called Niger, Lucius of Cyrene, Manaen (who had been brought up with Herod the tetrarch) and Saul." Notice that Luke lists not only these men's names, but also provides seemingly random facts. Actually, the specific details about each person listed speak volumes about their ethnicities.

Why was Simeon called Niger? Because Simeon was from Niger, located in sub-Saharan Africa, and likely Black as the very word, *niger*, means "black." Lucius was from Cyrene, a city near Africa's northern coast in what is today the country of Libya. There's also Manaen, who had grown up with Herod the tetrarch. This tells us that Manaen was from somewhere in Palestine—either Judea, Galilee, or perhaps even from Samaria—for the Herodian dynasty ruled over the entire region from approximately 65 BC to AD 90. Luke's comment about Manaen also points the reader to his privileged upbringing, for Manaen could not have been raised with a king's son unless he had the proper connections, pedigree, and access to funds. While this passage does not comment directly on the backgrounds of Barnabas or Paul, keep in mind there's no need to do so again. Luke had already informed his readers that Barnabas was from the island of Cyprus and Paul was from Tarsus, located in Asia Minor (Acts 4:36; 9:11).

Surely it is more than coincidental that two of the Antioch church leaders were from Africa, one was from the Mediterranean, one was from the Middle East, and one was from Asia Minor. Early church planters and believers reading this book would have clearly understood Luke's point: The local church should empower diverse leaders.

The early church was not only wrestling with issues of Gentile inclusion, but also with showing favoritism to those with economic means. James acknowledged this when he wrote:

> My brothers and sisters, believers . . . must not show favoritism. Suppose a man comes into your meeting wearing a gold ring and fine clothes, and a poor man in filthy old clothes also comes in. If you show special attention to the man wearing fine clothes and say, "Here's a good seat for you," but say to the poor man, "You stand there" or "Sit on the floor by my feet," have you not discriminated among yourselves . . . ? Listen: . . . Has not God [also] chosen those who are poor in the eyes of the world to be rich in faith and to inherit the kingdom he promised those who love him? But you have dishonored the poor. . . . If you really keep the royal law found in Scripture, "Love your neighbor as yourself," you are doing right. But if you show favoritism, you sin. (James 2:1–9)

Paul, too, taught that there are to be no distinctions in the body of Christ when he wrote, "So in Christ Jesus you are all children of God through faith, for all of you who were baptized into Christ have clothed yourselves with Christ. There is neither Jew nor Gentile, neither slave nor free, nor is there male and female, for you are all [equally] one in Christ Jesus" (Gal. 3:26–28).

Biblically informed, churches are expected to promote a spirit of inclusion that strategically accounts for the needs and concerns of everyone involved without showing preference for any one culture, class, or gender.

JOURNAL

Why do you think we naturally gravitate to what's comfortable?

What limits most churches from involving the poor, the homeless, or others of limited means, involvement, regular attendance, or active membership?

Think about your own church in this regard. Is it extending itself to the poor in ways that communicate love, value, and dignity in Christ? What barriers exist, or what subtle signals are being sent to those of limited means, that may be keeping them from feeling welcomed or getting involved?

DAY 2

HISTORY

The New Testament emphasizes the importance and necessity of the multiethnic church as a witness to the credibility of the gospel message. From the very beginning of church history, this has been the expectation. As mentioned in week one:

- Jesus *envisioned* the multiethnic church, for the sake of the gospel, on the night before he died (John 17:2–3, 20–23).
- Luke *described* the multiethnic church in action, at Antioch, as a model for future congregations to follow (Acts 11:19–26; 13:1–3).
- Paul *prescribed* the multiethnic church in order to advance a credible witness of God's love for all people (Eph. 2:11—4:6; 3:2, 6).

Today, in addition to what is otherwise biblical, pastors and sociologists alike recognize and affirm certain non-negotiable qualities as being fundamental to the design and development of a healthy multiethnic church. These are called the "Seven Core Commitments of a Healthy Multi-Ethnic Church."[1] Together with the biblical mandate summarized above, these commitments light the way for the emerging movement—the coming integration of the local church in America.

Seven core commitments of a multiethnic church are:

1. Embrace Dependence
2. Take Intentional Steps
3. Empower Diverse Leaders
4. Develop Cross-Cultural Relationships
5. Pursue Cross-Cultural Competence
6. Promote a Spirit of Inclusion
7. Mobilize for Impact

Over the next few days, we'll discuss each of these Seven Core Commitments (though not in this order) as we consider, "How Should the Church Respond?"

JOURNAL

· ● ● ● ·

Setting aside the Seven Core Commitments for a moment, what would you say is the most important thing a church can do to encourage greater diversity within its membership?

Are there barriers to instituting the answer you gave above at your church? What are they? How would you overcome them?

DAY 3

CONSIDERATIONS

Understanding the Seven Core Commitments essential to a multiethnic church transforms not just our church as a whole, but also each of us as individuals. To better understand these commitments, let's start with two key ones, vital concepts that can get a church moving quickly in the right direction.

EMBRACE DEPENDENCE

In Matthew 17:14–21, Jesus healed a young boy of seizures induced by a demon. When his disciples asked him, "Why couldn't we drive [the demon] out?" he replied, "Because you have so little faith." Mark 9:29 adds to the story, stating that Jesus then noted, "This kind can come out only by prayer."

Likewise, the multiethnic church is a different kind of church. In other words, there are no simple solutions, no shortcuts, and no strategies of humankind that can accomplish what only God can do in this regard. It is a work of the Holy Spirit and faith that cannot otherwise be attained through human means or efforts. Such a church can be established only when we commit ourselves to prayer, patience, and persistence in seeking to "walk [together as one with diverse others] in a manner worthy of the calling with which you [all] have been called" (Eph. 4:1 NASB).

TAKE INTENTIONAL STEPS

Intentionality requires both an attitude and an action that must permeate and inform every corridor of a healthy multiethnic church. For instance, there's little doubt that people mean well when they say they would gladly welcome people of various ethnic or economic backgrounds as a part of their church. However, in practice, what they really mean, often unknowingly, is, "as long as they like things the way we do them." Therefore, we should recognize that a healthy multiethnic church develops not by assimilation but rather by accommodation.

Notice the subtle difference in terminology. The word, *assimilate* means "to integrate somebody into a larger group so that differences are minimized or eliminated."[2] Yet the word, *accommodate* means "to adjust actions in response to somebody's needs."[3] This means you must not ask or expect diverse others to check their culture at the door in order to become part of your church. Rather, those in the majority are responsible to adjust their own attitudes and actions intentionally in order to enfold diverse others into the life of the growing, developing body. Likewise, minorities entering a different church culture should similarly approach the merger with prayer, patience, and persistence.

JOURNAL

. . ● . .

Many churches will be fearful of moving forward with accommodation because of the risk of losing current members. Given what you've discovered so far through this book, are you willing to commit yourself to developing a multiethnic church, even at the expense of your own personal preferences in worship or in other aspects of church life? Why or why not?

If the church you attend begins to accommodate other ethnicities, some of your friends might be uncomfortable with certain changes. What might you say to help a friend who expresses his or her frustration to you?

RELATIONSHIPS

With the right heart and attitude established by embracing dependence and becoming intentional in our actions, the next of the Seven Core Commitments calls us to begin reaching out to others.

DEVELOP CROSS-CULTURAL RELATIONSHIPS

It is true that some people have had legitimately negative encounters with people from other ethnicities or cultures, and that these experiences shaped their thoughts and feelings. Therefore, when attempting to encourage cross-cultural relationships within the local church, we should provide opportunities for open dialogue and commend those with both the courage to discuss such things, and the determination to deal with them. And when misunderstandings arise, we must determine, as in a marriage, to keep the ring on.

As director of cultural inclusion at my church, I (Oneya) have seen the beauty of diverse relationships as they bring faith, hope, and healing to many people, time and again. Perhaps it's these unlikely friendships, once established, that bless me the most. Multiethnic churches are perfect environments to foster cross-cultural relationships.

For example, two women, one Black and one White, recently took our church's cultural competence class. After some initial trepidation, they began to open up and share their stories and life experiences with one another. Soon, they became more than classmates; they became genuinely interested in one another as friends and sisters in Christ. For them, meeting for coffee is now routine. Even four hours together, I'm told, is not long enough!

Pastors, too, gain credibility with diverse congregants when they take time to understand the experience of others. When I first met my pastor, Chris Beard, for instance, he already knew why African Americans (especially older ones) never leave a store without putting their purchases in a bag. And he understood the rules that Black men are taught to follow when stopped by the police. When I asked Chris how he, being White, knew of such things, he explained that he had sought out respected African-American pastors to disciple him in cross-cultural competence. As an African-American woman, that impressed me, and for over ten years I've called Peoples Church home.

For these and other reasons, churches everywhere should encourage and provide cross-cultural education and opportunities for their members to grow, whether formally or informally, in this regard. Such education leads to greater health in the body and will mitigate unnecessary conflict in the long run between diverse attenders who do not otherwise know or understand one another.

JOURNAL

• ◦ ● ◦ •

Why is it necessary to be intentional about developing cross-cultural relationships rather than waiting for them to happen naturally?

As you intentionally build cross-cultural relationships, God will increase your sensitivity to the attitudes of your heart. What should a person do with prejudicial thoughts and feelings when they arise?

Describe how you have grown from and/or contributed to any cross-cultural relationships that you've had to date?

COMMUNICATION

Multiethnic churches and individuals need to move beyond establishing strong interpersonal relationships among various groups of people. They must invite diverse people into leadership and mobilize the groups toward unity and kingdom impact—the next two core commitments.

EMPOWER DIVERSE LEADERS

Churches must also empower diverse vocational and volunteer leaders, from the pulpit to the nursery and at every station in between. Indeed, credibility and modeling in a multiethnic church begins here. However, it's important to recognize that when it comes to staffing, intentionality is the middle ground between quota and wishful thinking. Churches should not force the issue by predetermining just which or how many different kinds of people they will empower as leaders at a given moment. God must be involved in the process. On the other hand, churches seeking to become increasingly diverse must do more than simply hope and pray that a well-qualified candidate of varied ethnic origin will somehow appear at the door!

If you're in a position of leadership, keep your eyes open and become ever more aware of the wonderfully diverse people God is putting in your path. Indeed, there are many gifted leaders in every people group just waiting to be asked, trained, and deployed for service.

With leadership in mind, it's critical that the vision to become a multi-ethnic church is understood, embraced, and communicated clearly to others by those in charge. "Clergy have come to see the church as an institution for challenging [people] to new hopes and new visions of a better world. Laity, on the other hand, are in large part committed to the view that the church should be a source of comfort for them in a troubled world."[4] Therefore the vision for change, especially uncomfortable change, must come from the top.

MOBILIZE FOR IMPACT

The intended outcome of establishing a multiethnic church is not unity for unity's sake. Rather, it is to turn the power and pleasure of God—uniquely expressed in a church where diverse people "are being built together to become a dwelling in which God lives by his Spirit" (Eph. 2:22)—outward in order to bless the broader community, lead people to Christ, encourage the greater body, and fulfill the Great Commission (Matt. 28:19–20). In the future, to win the world for Jesus we must speak with one voice, one heart, and one message. And through multiethnic churches, we can do just that as we diligently proclaim and "preserve the unity of the Spirit in the bond of peace. [For] there is one body and one Spirit, just as also you were called in one hope of your calling; one Lord, one faith, one baptism, one God and Father of all who is over all and through all and in all" (Eph. 4:3–6 NASB).

In addition, a healthy multiethnic church also focuses on kingdom work as a way to help its diverse members build relational bonds. For instance, it's easier for a church that promotes evangelism to be multiethnic because its members commit themselves to a kingdom work far greater than their differences. Churches whose cross-cultural engagement remains strictly social in focus will find integrating across racial lines much more difficult. By embracing a common cause, however, people naturally will grow together as they "go" together.

By focusing on kingdom work, a multiethnic church communicates a credible witness of the gospel to its community and its city. As others see us walking, working, and worshiping God together as one, and addressing the needs of others beyond race and class distinctions, the multiethnic church becomes a powerful witness of God's love for all people. In turn, it will be greatly appreciated by people—even those who do not yet believe as we do.

JOURNAL

• • • • •

Research the demographics of the zip code in which your church is located. You can easily find this information on the web at www.city-data.com. What is the racial/ethnic makeup in the zip code by percentages? What is the median income of the zip code compared to the median income in your state?

Now consider the demographics within your own church. Do they mirror the diversity of its community? Is this a positive or a negative in your view?

Go to your church's web page and, if possible, look at the vocational staff team. Does the team reflect the diversity of the community in which the church is established, of the congregation, or of both? What does this say about your church and its understanding of the multiethnic vision?

COMPETENCE

The final two of the Seven Core Commitments address the mastery of a cross-cultural "skill set" and the importance of developing a spirit of inclusivity. Together, these allow our heart for others to shine, and they convey to diverse others that we as individuals, and as a church, welcome them into our lives.

PURSUE CROSS-CULTURAL COMPETENCE

The understanding necessary to successfully navigate a cross-cultural environment is gained through experience and interaction with diverse people, especially those with whom we are one in the Lord. In this way, we gradually develop cross-cultural competence. As mentioned in week one, in this context, *competence* refers to proficiency in addressing another's culture or customs, needs, and expectations when they differ from our own. It means becoming adept in the idiosyncrasies of language and learning the ins and outs of the traditions of others. Once acquired, cross-cultural competence allows us to interact in a more informed and effective way with people of varying ethnic or economic backgrounds. In many ways, cross-cultural competence is more caught than taught.

Although competence does not assume expertise, it does describe a general aptitude in working with people of diverse cultures. More specifically, it defines individuals who "value diversity, conduct self-assessment, manage the dynamics of difference, acquire and institutionalize cultural knowledge, and are able to adapt to diversity and the cultural contexts of the communities they serve."[5]

Pursuit of cross-cultural competence moves us beyond ourselves toward a deeper understanding of life from another's perspective. Such insights should draw us nearer to others who are not like us and, as we bond and grow together with them, nearer to Christ in and through the local church. The fact is, church leaders can no longer afford to be cross-culturally incompetent in an increasingly interconnected world.

PROMOTE A SPIRIT OF INCLUSION

Two thousand years ago Paul commanded the church at Philippi to "do nothing from selfishness or empty conceit, but with humility of mind regard one another as more important than yourselves; do not *merely* look out for your own personal interests, but also for the interests of others" (Phil. 2:3–4 NASB). In other words, Paul expected individuals in a congregation to not just look inward but to get beyond themselves for the benefit of others.

His words should inspire present-day attitudes and approaches that foster local church environments in which diverse people will not only feel welcomed, but will also become a significant part of the whole. Believers who embrace this imperative will discover they can worship God joyfully even at times, for example, when the music played on a Sunday morning does not reflect their own personal tastes, when someone prays in a language they do not understand, or when other things do not match their preferences.

To promote an inclusive spirit, churches must also pay attention to those little things that add up to create the look and feel of the whole. At Mark's church, Mosaic in Little Rock, Arkansas, for example, signage is produced in both English and Spanish, as are the bulletins and PowerPoint slides. And flags that fly from the ceiling represent the diversity of nations within the body. Such considerations, though seemingly inconsequential, demonstrate to others a great deal about who the church is and what it values. A spirit of inclusion means inviting diversity into the big things as well. If people of color are included in your signage decisions, but have no real ability to influence your church, they will ultimately feel excluded. Including others means sharing power as well as accommodating culture.

However, a commitment to promote a spirit of inclusion in no way implies a commitment to embrace doctrines or practices that, in one way or another, violates God's Word. Ultimately, the goal is to create an environment where all people feel welcome, where truth is proclaimed, and where grace and mercy abound.

JOURNAL

• • ● • •

What is one thing you have learned recently that's improved your own cross-cultural competence?

Next Sunday at church, pick out someone who is ethnically or economically different than you and try to observe the entire experience from his or her point of view. List the things that promote a spirit of inclusion and things that may seem insensitive, exclusive, or even just confusing to him or her. We'll consider this further next week.

REFLECTION

As you read the following verses, ask the Lord to speak to your heart through them, based on what you've been learning.

Then Jesus said to his host, "When you give a luncheon or dinner, do not invite your friends, your brothers or sisters, your relatives, or your rich neighbors; if you do, they may invite you back and so you will be repaid. But when you give a banquet, invite the poor, the crippled, the lame, the blind, and you will be blessed. Although they cannot repay you, you will be repaid at the resurrection of the righteous." (Luke 14:12–14)

As He was setting out on a journey, a man ran up to Him and knelt before Him, and asked Him, "Good Teacher, what shall I do to inherit eternal life?" And Jesus said to him, "Why do you call Me good? No one is good except God alone. You know the commandments, 'DO NOT MURDER, DO NOT COMMIT ADULTERY, DO NOT STEAL, DO NOT BEAR FALSE WITNESS, Do not defraud, HONOR YOUR FATHER AND MOTHER.'" And he said to Him, "Teacher, I have kept all these things from my youth up." Looking at him, Jesus felt a love for him and said to him, "One thing you lack: go and sell all you possess and give to the poor, and you will have treasure in heaven; and come, follow Me."

But at these words he was saddened, and he went away grieving, for he was one who owned much property. (Mark 10:17–22 NASB)

JOURNAL

· · ● · ·

Write a prayer inspired by the verses you just read.

WEEK 8

LIVING A MULTIETHNIC
CHRISTIAN LIFE

· · ● · ·

THEOLOGY

The heart of a community is transformed not by education or by legislation, but through reconciliation—a ministry given to and expected of the local church. In fact, the apostle Paul made this clear when speaking to the church at Corinth. As you read the following passage, note that *all* means "all" (including diverse people).

> For the love of Christ controls us, having concluded this, that one died for all, therefore all died; and He died for all, so that they who live might no longer live for themselves, but for Him who died and rose again on their behalf. . . . Now all *these* things are from God, who reconciled us to Himself through Christ and gave us the ministry of reconciliation, namely, that God was in Christ reconciling the world to Himself, not counting their trespasses against them, and He has committed to us the word of reconciliation. Therefore, we are ambassadors for Christ, as though God were making an appeal through us; we beg you on behalf of Christ, be reconciled to God. (2 Cor. 5:14–15, 18–20 NASB)

Let's break this down.

Notice first that the entire section begins with an expectation; namely, that Christ's love will control us (in the Greek, *synecho*, meaning "to hold together"). And just who is *us*? Paul was speaking not so much of individuals here, but of a corporate body; in this case, the local church at Corinth. Not only does Christ's love hold us all together (in Christ and in the church), it compels us to live for ourselves no longer.

Understanding that Christ died for all people—that is, one new people he would bring together—and not just for the Jews (Col. 3:9–15), Paul stated that Christ has given to us (the church) the ministry of reconciliation. This ministry, he explained, will be advanced not only through the "word of reconciliation" (the preaching of the gospel), but through our collective witness as ambassadors of Christ when we walk, work, and worship God together as one, beyond the divisive distinctions of this world. Through unity and diversity we advance the ministry of reconciliation—man to God and man to man—in and through the local church. As we do, we present a credible and compelling witness to others: "Come, be reconciled to God with us."

JOURNAL

• • ● • •

Typically, Christians assume that the ministry of reconciliation is limited to reconciling men and women to God through faith in Jesus Christ. But in living for him who died and rose again, make an argument for why it should or should not extend to reconciling diverse men and women to one another as well.

Why might Paul have connected reconciliation with God and reconciliation among people? What does one have to do with the other?

DAY 2
HISTORY

Who is my neighbor? Israeli and Palestinian, Hutu and Tutsi, Sunni and Shiite. These modern conflicts give us an idea of the deep-seated enmity between Jews and Gentiles during the time of Christ. However, when Jesus encountered the divide he did not avoid it, as we are prone to do. Rather, he stepped into it with purpose in order to break down barriers and promote reconciliation. He was also purposeful in helping bridge divides between Jews and "undesirables" of the day, such as he did with a Samaritan woman and with tax collectors in general (John 4:1–42).

One of the clearest, yet most overlooked, interactions of Christ with Gentiles occurred when he fed the four thousand (Mark 8:1–21). This account comes just two chapters after a similar feeding of five thousand (Mark 6:30–44). It's important to note that this first miracle occurred in a Jewish area. The twelve baskets of bread that were left over symbolized that in Christ there was more than enough for all twelve tribes from the nation of Israel.

Having witnessed this miracle, the disciples would have understood Jesus' heart for all people; or so one would think. But consider their conversation with him in Mark 8:2–4: [Jesus said,] "I have compassion for these people; they have already been with me three days and have nothing to eat. If I send them home hungry, they will collapse on the way, because some of them have come a long distance." His disciples answered, "But where in this remote place can anyone get enough bread to feed them?"

Typically, the disciples' response in this passage is attributed to their lack of faith. However, as we read the New Testament in view of Christ's ministry of reconciliation, we see another potential, or at least contributing, cause. Jesus had just miraculously multiplied fish and loaves, so why would they doubt he could do it again? Perhaps the disciples were asking, "Are you really going to do a miracle for these (Gentile) people?"

By feeding the four thousand, in the region of Decapolis, where Gentiles were certainly present, Jesus answered this question with a decisive "Yes!" And after this mealtime miracle, not twelve but seven baskets of bread were left over. In the ancient world, the number seven often symbolized all of the people groups and nations of the world. In fact, it's been suggested that by performing the same miracle at a gathering of both Jews and Gentiles, Jesus was illustrating that there is more than enough of him for the entire world.

In living a multiethnic Christian life, remember that Jesus has gone before us to show us the way—not only in salvation, but also in reconciliation between God and man.

JOURNAL

• • ● • •

Mark 5:1–20 and 7:31–37 records some other times when Jesus interacted with Gentiles. Read these passages and notice the people's reaction to Jesus' miraculous work among them.

What light do these other examples shed on the Syrophoenician woman's response of faith in Christ in Mark 7:24–30?

CONSIDERATIONS

In most cases, it's easy to love those closest to us: family, friends, and those with whom we have things in common. But Christ expects more of us than loving only those who are like us. Admittedly, it's much easier to attend church with those who share our ethnic heritage, economic status, or any number of other similarities. Yet we should remember that God gives no pass for degree of difficulty in the Bible when it comes to fulfilling his will as individuals or in our churches. Instead, he provides all we need to accomplish it.

In following Christ we've been called to live in the supernatural, above and beyond what is otherwise natural, for God's glory and not our own. And while it's true that people most often choose a church to attend based on what they like about it, we should ask: Is it really about us and what we like? Rather, the will of God should inform our decisions, not simply (or worse yet, selfishly) our will.

As I (Mark) consider my current church and the characteristics God has given it to make it impactful, any measure of influence or significance that it has had to date is not due to the size of our ministry, but due to its scope and influence. Any impact has come not because we have drawn large numbers of people, but because we have attracted diverse people from the community who willingly set aside personal preferences to walk as one for the sake of the gospel. As you might imagine, this is not easy for them to do given that there are many more comfortable and convenient churches to attend in Little Rock.

Truth be told, I personally prefer a large church setting. In fact, I left a homogeneous church of five thousand people to start Mosaic. Yet there's something interesting I've come to realize when comparing a homogeneous church to a multiethnic church in terms of potential influence. When the five thousand or so similar people of my former church leave on a Sunday morning, they head back to largely the same neighborhoods and work environments, the same athletic facilities and country clubs, and the same schools and social settings. But when the five hundred or so diverse people of Mosaic leave on Sunday morning, they spread out to permeate every nook and cranny of the city. The homeless return to the streets, while other members return to homes in the hoods, the barrios, the suburbs, and everywhere else in between. Many of our immigrant members work in the service industry and in construction, while other members hold political office. From hospitals to corporate boardrooms, from maids to small business owners and nonprofit CEOs, the ethnic and economic diversity of our membership provides a much broader presence and influence in the community than our size might otherwise suggest.

So whether you are a part of a large, medium, or small congregation, know that your pursuit of a church that reflects the community's diversity matters to God and to your city. No matter what its size, it will be the people and passion of such a church that others find compelling.

JOURNAL

∘ ∘ ● ∘ ∘

What church do you currently attend and why? List the top two or three reasons you chose this particular church as your own.

How does the church you currently attend fit with your desire to grow in your understanding of what it means to live a multiethnic Christian life?

DAY 4
RELATIONSHIPS

Throughout the past eight weeks, you've considered living a multiethnic Christian life. But have you entered into any new cross-cultural relationships, or have any existing ones further developed as a result? To answer this question, respond again to the My Personal Experience Survey in this section.

This time, as you retake the survey, visualize the specific names and faces of those to whom each question may apply. Think also about the stage in which these relationships exist based on Witherspoon's cross-cultural worship model (CCW) that we discussed in week six. If you need to remind yourself of the specifics of his model, return to day four of week six. There you learned that cross-cultural relationships are either fixed or moving in the following direction:

Integration $\longrightarrow$ Penetration $\longrightarrow$ Reconciliation

With this in mind, and in checking a particular box below, write an (I), a (P), or an (R) next to your mark (X) to describe the stage in which you believe the relationship currently exists. For example, see line one below.

MY PERSONAL EXPERIENCE SURVEY
Check the boxes that apply to you.

Personal Experiences	Whites	Blacks	Asians	Latinos	Others
I have worked on teams with		X		X R	
I have worked for					

MY PERSONAL EXPERIENCE SURVEY
Check the boxes that apply to you.

Personal Experiences	Whites	Blacks	Asians	Latinos	Others
I have worked on teams with					
I have worked for					
I have managed					
I have gone to lunch with					
I have sought out for personal advice					
I have been mentored by					
I have spent time discussing my faith with					
I have had in my home as part of a larger group					
I have had in my home as individuals or a family					
I have seen films about					
I have read books about					
My children regularly play with					
I grew up in a neighborhood with					
My current neighbors include					
My social circles include					
I have close friends who are					
I have taken a vacation with					
I have had in my home overnight					
I have been discriminated by					
I have been criminally victimized by					
I have been emotionally hurt by					

JOURNAL

• • ● • •

Compare your responses in the survey here with those from week one. Has there been any significant change since week one in your responses? If so, describe what has occurred and why.

In which area(s) are you most lacking in terms of developing cross-cultural relationships or understanding?

Pick one area and consider when, how, and with whom it can improve. Toward that end, what action might you take?

DAY 5
COMMUNICATION

Being able to share or otherwise communicate to others the things you have learned through this study is an important part of completing it. With this in mind, we want to help you prepare for such an opportunity in the future. Today you'll create an action plan with what we'll call SMART goals, which can help leaders in your own church pursue the multiethnic vision for the sake of the gospel.

To explain, SMART goals are:

Specific, not vague.
Measurable, having a clear goal indicating it has been achieved.
Attainable, can be achieved.
Realistic, not miraculous.
Timely, meeting both real and felt needs.

Now imagine that your church tasked you to help it become a healthy multiethnic congregation of faith by developing SMART goals and the action steps it will need to take in order to achieve them.

Remember, taking action and moving others toward change in a church can be complicated. Therefore, you'll not only need to set goals but also be able to communicate your plan to church leaders in a way that is both clear and compelling. Your suggestions will be incredibly important and may very well set your church on a path that will lead to the salvation and life change of many people in the years ahead!

Begin this exercise by reflecting on what you've learned over the past eight weeks and the insights you've gained into your own church.

JOURNAL

Ask yourself: What should my church look and feel like in terms of its diversity?

Think about what you have observed recently at your church as you have considered things from the perspective of diverse others. What are some of your most important thoughts and conclusions? Write them down here.

What are three SMART goals you can recommend to church leaders in order to help them plant, grow, or further develop a healthy multiethnic church?

SMART goal number 1:

SMART goal number 2:

SMART goal number 3:

Write a thoughtful summary and explanation of your three goals, their rationale, and a suggested plan for action.

Once you do, prayerfully determine with whom, when, and how to share your summary (for example: in person, via e-mail, or through a formal letter). Please note, when sharing with church leaders, be positive (use the sandwich conversation approach), staying mindful that not everything you suggest may be embraced or implemented. Remember, similar to sharing your faith, results are out of your control. Nevertheless, pray and believe that God will reward your heart and effort.

If you have been going through this study with a small group, write and share the summary together.

COMPETENCE

Once a man, seeking to justify himself, asked Jesus, "What must I do to inherit eternal life?" Jesus responded, "'Love the Lord your God with all your heart'... and 'Love your neighbor as yourself'" (Luke 10:25–27). Jesus then told a parable, the story of the good Samaritan (see v. 29).

To fully understand the parable, it's important to recall that Samaritans were the descendants of the northern kingdom of Jews conquered by the Assyrians in 722 BC. Over time, the once pure Jewish bloodline in the North was corrupted through intermarriage. Worship of Yahweh, too, was corrupted through the assimilation of pagan beliefs and ritual. Consequently, devout Jews living in Judea (the southern kingdom) at the time of Christ wanted nothing to do with Samaritans.

The primary purpose of the parable was to clarify just whom Jesus had in mind in speaking of a neighbor. In other words, it was to answer the question, "Who is my neighbor?" Therefore, through the parable, Jesus explained that a neighbor is not only someone in need, but includes those we might tend to avoid, disregard, or even despise, based on ethnic origin or other characteristics. Practically speaking, the implication for the man listening to Jesus was that he would have to learn not only to love God and others but particularly others unlike himself, without distinction, in order to fulfill God's will. We must learn to do so as well.

So, ask yourself:

* When was the last time you invited a neighbor to your house for dinner, to spend an evening out, or to visit your church?
* What is the one thing you remember most about your time together?

In addition to creating SMART goals for your church and sharing them with church leaders, you should also create goals for yourself personally and share them with a friend or accountability partner. Depending on whom you choose to share your goals with, any number of purposes may be served. For instance:

* If you share them with someone of a different ethnicity, he or she might help to mentor you in pursuit of cross-cultural competence.
* If you share them with someone of your own ethnicity, someone perhaps not as far along in their understanding of such things as you, you may inspire their own thinking and desires as well.

No matter whom you choose to share with, your actions matter. Whether you help to move your own church along, or a friend, be assured that in doing so you are helping to advance the kingdom of God on earth, so it will be as it will one day be in heaven . . . when distinctions will no longer divide us but enhance our love for one another and for our Lord and Savior, Jesus Christ.

JOURNAL

Throughout this study, you may have encountered some uncomfortable truths. Now is the time to cement your forward progress. Take a moment to set three SMART goals for you to accomplish personally in the next three months as you pursue a multiethnic Christian life. These goals should include at least one item having to do with the broader community, such as petitioning the government on an issue of injustice or joining a board to oversee educational improvements in your city. Pursuit of positive change must be focused both on an individual improvement and collective (structural) improvement.

SMART goal number 1:

SMART goal number 2:

SMART goal number 3:

Write down the name of someone with whom you can share these goals and who can help hold you accountable to fulfil them.

Call to make an appointment with this person within the next two weeks. Write down the time and place you will meet.

REFLECTION

As you read the following verses, ask the Lord to speak to your heart through them, based on what you've been learning.

Have this attitude in yourselves that was also in Christ Jesus, who, although He existed in the form of God, did not regard equality with God a thing to be grasped, but emptied Himself, taking the form of a bond-servant, *and* being made in the likeness of men. Being found in appearance as a man, He humbled Himself by becoming obedient to the point of death, even death on a cross. For this reason also, God highly exalted Him, and bestowed on Him the name which is above every name, so that at the name of Jesus EVERY KNEE WILL BOW, of those who are in heaven and on earth and under the earth, and that every tongue will confess that Jesus Christ is Lord, to the glory of God the Father. (Phil. 2:5–11 NASB)

After this I looked, and there before me was a great multitude that no one could count, from every nation, tribe, people and language, standing before the throne and before the Lamb. They were wearing White robes and were holding palm branches in their hands. And they cried out in a loud voice: "Salvation belongs to our God, who sits on the throne, and to the Lamb." (Rev. 7:9–10)

JOURNAL

• • ● • •

Write a prayer inspired by the verses you just read. As the study draws to a close, consider making it a benediction.

NOTES

WEEK 1

1. John McManners, ed., *The Oxford Illustrated History of Christianity* (Oxford: Oxford University Press, 1990), 407.

2. "Demographics of the United States," *Wikipedia*, accessed June 7, 2016, http://en.wikipedia.org/wiki/Demographics_of_the_United_States.

3. Kristin Deasy, "Whites to Be Minority in America in 2043: Census," *GlobalPost* (December 2012). http://www.globalpost.com/dispatch/news/regions/americas/united-states/121212/whites-be-minority-america-2043-census.

4. Frank Bass, "Census Bureau Says Minority Youth to Be Majority by 2019," *Bloomberg* (December 2012). http://www.bloomberg.com/news/2012-12-12/census-bureau-says-minority-youth-to-be-majority-by-2019.html.

5. Michael O. Emerson and Christian Smith, *Divided by Faith: Evangelical Religion and the Problem of Race in America* (New York: Oxford University Press, 2000).

6. Sir William Macpherson of Cluny, *The Stephen Lawrence Inquiry* (1999), para. 6:34. https://www.gov.uk/government/uploads/system/uploads/attachment_data/file/277111/4262.pdf.

7. Bonita Williams, "Accomplishing Cross Cultural Competence in Youth Development Programs," *Journal of Extension*, 39, no. 6 (December 2001). http://www.joe.org/joe/2001december/ iw1.php.

WEEK 2

1. Yamiche Alcindor and Larry Copeland, "After Zimmerman Verdict, Can Nation Heal Racial Rift?" *USA Today* (July 2013). www.usatoday.com/story/news/nation/2013/07/14/nation-moves-forward-after-zimmerman-trial-2516189/.

2. "Spontaneous Comments to the Press," Barack Obama (July 2013). https://www.whitehouse.gov/the-press-office/2013/07/19/remarks-president-trayvon-martin.

3. John M. Perkins, "Irresistibly Fish" (September 2013). https://brett fish.word press.com/2013/09/12/ccda-conference-in-new-orleans-2013-cultivate-the-soul-day-2-the-a-m/.

4. David T. Olsen, presentation at the National Multiethnic Church Conference, San Diego, CA (November 2011). For more information, see http://www.theamerican church.org.

5. Ibid.

6. Ibid.

7. Ibid.

8. Ibid.

9. Bob Sullivan and Hugh Thompson, "Now Hear This! Most People Stink at Listening," *Scientific American* (May 2013). http://www.scientificamerican.com/article.cfm?id= plateau-effect-digital-gadget-distraction-attention.

10. Pew Research Center, "Beyond Distrust: How Americans View Their Government" (November 2015). www.people-press.org/2015/11/23/beyond-distrust-how-americans-view-their-government/.

11. Joshua Bickel, "How the Faithful Voted: 2012 Preliminary Analysis," *Pew Research Center* (November 2012). http://www.pew forum.org/2012/11/07/how-the-faithful-voted-2012-preliminary-exit-poll-analysis/.

WEEK 3

1. John McManners, ed., *The Oxford Illustrated History of Christianity* (Oxford: Oxford University Press, 1990), 423.

2. Michael O. Emerson and George Yancey, *Transcending Racial Barriers: Toward a Mutual Obligations Approach* (New York: Oxford University Press, 2011), 18.

3. Ian H. López, *White By Law: The Legal Construction of Race* (New York: New York University Press, 2006), 3.

4. Image modified from Gary R. Weaver, ed., *Culture, Communication and Conflict: Readings in Intercultural Relations*, second edition (New York: Simon and Schuster Publishing, 1998). https://home.snu.edu/~hculbert/iceberg.htm.

5. Efrem Smith, *The Post-Black and Post-White Church: Becoming the Beloved Community in a Multi-Ethnic World* (San Francisco: Jossey-Bass, 2012), 107.

6. Chul Tim Chang, *Korean Ethnic Church Growth Phenomenon in the United States* (Claremont, CA: American Academy of Religion, 2006), 3.

WEEK 4

1. To see how Paul's teaching concerning the mystery of Christ is typically misunderstood and misapplied by American evangelicals, see Dan Delzell, "Do You Understand the Mystery of Christ?" *The Christian Post* (September 2013). http://www.christian post.com/news/do-you-understand-the-mystery-of-christ-103858.

2. For more concerning the proper understanding of the mystery of Christ, see Mark DeYmaz, "Understanding the Mystery of Christ," *The Christian Post* (September 2013). http://www.christianpost.com/news/understanding-the-mystery-of-christ-104745/.

3. Dwight N. Hopkins, *Down, Up, and Over: Slave Religion and Black Theology* (Minneapolis: Augsburg Fortress, 2000), 19.

4. Ibid., 32.

5. Ibid., 33.

6. Howard Dodson, "How Slavery Helped Build a World Economy," *National Geographic* (February 2003). http://news.nationalgeographic.com/news/2003/01/0131_030203_jubilee2.html.

7. US Census, 1860.

8. Michael O. Emerson and Christian Smith, *Divided by Faith: Evangelical Religion and the Problem of Race in America* (New York: Oxford University Press, 2000), 9.

9. Ibid., 7.

10. Jeff Stone, et al. "Stereotype Threat Effects on Black and White Athletic Performance," *Journal of Personality and Social Psychology*, 77 (December 1999), 1217.

11. Garry Wills, *Under God: Religion and American Politics* (New York: Simon and Schuster, 1990), 198.

12. Ibid., 199.

13. Jack Niemonen, *Race, Class, and the State in Contemporary Sociology* (Boulder, CO: Lynne Rienner Publishers Inc., 2002), 204.

14. Joseph Daniels, "The Psychopathology of Racism," *Christianity Today*, January 1971, 7–8 (qtd. by Emerson and Smith).

15. Virginia Ramey Mollenkott, "Up from Ignorance: Awareness-Training and Racism," *Christianity Today* 15:6–8 (qtd. by Emerson and Smith).

WEEK 5

1. What follows here was first brought to light in Mark DeYmaz and Harry Li, *Leading a Healthy Multi-Ethnic Church* (Grand Rapids, MI: Zondervan, 2010), 79–81.

2. Ibid., 220–221.

3. Ibid., 16.

4. Ibid., 28.

5. Faith Communities Today, "FACTs On Growth: 2010," *Faith Communities Today* (December 2011). http://faithcommunitiestoday.org/fact-2010.

6. Scott Thumma, "Racial Diversity Increasing In U.S. Congregations," *The Huffington Post* (March 2013). http://www.huffingtonpost.com/scott-thumma-phd/racial-diversity-increasing-in-us-congregations_b_2944470.html.

7. Ibid.

8. Spencer Perkins and Chris Rice, *More Than Equals: Racial Healing for the Sake of the Gospel* (Downers Grove, IL: InterVarsity Press, 1993), 261.

9. Scott Williams, *Church Diversity: Sunday the Most Segregated Day of the Week* (Green Forest, AR: New Leaf Press, 2011), 43.

10. Barry Hankins, *American Evangelicals: A Contemporary History of a Mainstream Religious Movement* (Lanham, MD: Rowan and Littlefield Publishers, 2008), 129.

WEEK 6

1. Joshua Bickel, "How the Faithful Voted: 2012 Preliminary Analysis," *Pew Research Center* (November 2012). http://www.pewforum.org/ 2012/11/07/how-the-faithful-voted-2012-preliminary-exit-poll-analysis/.

2. Ibid.

3. Ibid.

4. Michael O. Emerson and Christian Smith, *Divided by Faith: Evangelical Religion and the Problem of Race in America* (New York: Oxford University Press, 2000), 97.

5. Ibid.

6. Barron Witherspoon Sr., *The Fallacy of Affinity* (Indianapolis: Dog Ear Publishing, 2010), 67.

7. Ibid., 73.

8. Ibid., 78.

9. Napp Nazworth, "How Multi-Ethnic Churches Could Help Close the Race Wage Gap," *Christian Post* (August 2013). http://www.christianpost.com/news/how- multi-ethnic-churches-could-help-close-the-race-wage-gap-101292/.

10. Rakesh Kochhar, Richard Fry, and Paul Taylor, "Wealth Gaps Rise to Record Highs Between Whites, Blacks, Hispanics" *Pew Research Center* (July 2011). http://www.pewsocialtrends.org/2011/07/26/wealth-gaps-rise-to-record-highs-between-whites-blacks-hispanics/.

11. Ibid.

WEEK 7

1. The biblical mandate and Seven Core Commitments were first described by Mark DeYmaz, in *Building a Healthy Multi-Ethnic Church* (San Francisco: Jossey-Bass, 2007). Each of the subsequent descriptions in this chapter has been drawn from Mark DeYmaz and Harry Li, *Leading a Healthy Multi-Ethnic Church* (formerly *Ethnic Blends* [Grand Rapids, MI: Zondervan, 2013]).

2. *Microsoft Encarta College Dictionary* (New York: St. Martin's Press, 2001), s. v. "assimilate."

3. Ibid., s. v. "accommodate."

4. Jeffery Hadden, *The Gathering Storm in the Churches* (New York: Doubleday, 1969), 206-207 (qtd. by Emerson and Smith).

5. "Definitions of Cultural Competence," National Center for Cultural Competence (1998). http://www.nccccurricula.info/culturalcompetence.html.

ABOUT THE AUTHORS

Dr. Mark DeYmaz (D.Min) is the founding pastor and directional leader of the Mosaic Church of Central Arkansas, and the co-founder and president of the Mosaix Global Network. His books include *Building a Healthy Multi-Ethnic Church,* which was chosen as a finalist for a *Christianity Today* Book of the Year Award and for a Resource of the Year Award sponsored by *Outreach* magazine (2008); *Leading a Healthy Multi-Ethnic Church; re:MIX: Transitioning Your Church to Living Color;* and *Disruption: Repurposing the Church to Redeem the Community.*

Oneya Fennell Okuwobi serves as the director of cultural inclusion at Peoples Church (Cincinnati, OH), which has transitioned from a 98 percent White commuter church to a church that reflects the diversity of the city (25 percent African American, 25 percent other minorities and internationals, and 50 percent White). She also directs City Cohorts for the Mosaix Global Network. Oneya is currently pursuing a PhD in sociology, focused on race and religion, at The Ohio State University.